T0319107

Cambridge Elements ≡

Elements in the History of Constantinople
edited by
Peter Frankopan
University of Oxford

THE STATUES OF CONSTANTINOPLE

Albrecht Berger
Ludwig Maximilian University of Munich

CAMBRIDGE
UNIVERSITY PRESS

CAMBRIDGE
UNIVERSITY PRESS

University Printing House, Cambridge CB2 8BS, United Kingdom

One Liberty Plaza, 20th Floor, New York, NY 10006, USA

477 Williamstown Road, Port Melbourne, VIC 3207, Australia

314–321, 3rd Floor, Plot 3, Splendor Forum, Jasola District Centre,
New Delhi – 110025, India

103 Penang Road, #05–06/07, Visioncrest Commercial, Singapore 238467

Cambridge University Press is part of the University of Cambridge.

It furthers the University's mission by disseminating knowledge in the pursuit of
education, learning, and research at the highest international levels of excellence.

www.cambridge.org
Information on this title: www.cambridge.org/9781108958370
DOI: 10.1017/9781108956147

© Albrecht Berger 2021

First published 2021

A catalogue record for this publication is available from the British Library.

ISBN 978-1-108-95837-0 Paperback
ISSN 2514-3891 (online)
ISSN 2514-3883 (print)

The Statues of Constantinople

Elements in the History of Constantinople

DOI: 10.1017/9781108956147
First published online: June 2021

Albrecht Berger
Ludwig Maximilian University of Munich
Author for correspondence: Albrecht Berger, albrecht.berger@lmu.de

Abstract: This Element discusses the ancient statues once set up in Byzantine Constantinople, with a special focus on their popular reception. From its foundation by Constantine the Great in 324, Constantinople housed a great number of statues which stood in the city on streets and public places, or were kept in several collections and in the Hippodrome. Almost all of them, except a number of newly made statues of reigning emperors, were ancient objects which had been brought to the city from other places. Many of these statues were later identified with persons other than those they actually represented, or received an allegorical (sometimes even an apocalyptical) interpretation. When the Crusaders of the Fourth Crusade conquered the city in 1204, almost all of the statues of Constantinople were destroyed or looted.

Keywords: Constantinople, Byzantine age, ancient Greek art, statues, popular reception

ISBNs: 9781108958370 (PB), 9781108956147 (OC)
ISSNs: 2514-3891 (online), 2514-3883 (print)

Contents

Contents

1 Introduction

Constantinople was a city of statues, from its foundation in 324 to the conquest by the Crusaders at the Fourth Crusade in 1204. Most of these statues were not, however, works of the Byzantine age but objects of ancient art, and therefore represented an older layer of culture in general and a real or imagined local history in particular.[1]

Almost none of these statues have survived to our day. Most of them were destroyed in the course of time, and only a few still exist in Western Europe as spoils of the Crusaders' conquest of Constantinople in 1204, such as the well-known porphyry sculpture of the four Tetrarchs and the four bronze horses now at Saint Mark's in Venice, or the bronze statue of an emperor (probably that of Emperor Leon I (457–74) from his column on the acropolis of Byzantium) which stands today before the cathedral of Barletta in southern Italy. In Istanbul no major ancient bronze object has survived until today except the Serpent column in the Hippodrome,[2] while the few small statues of stone that have been found there, mostly in a fragmentary state, do not belong to those mentioned by the sources.[3]

Pictures from the Byzantine age showing the statues of Constantinople and other places are very rare, and those we have are mostly conventionalised to a degree which makes them worthless for understanding the statues' real appearance. To talk about the statues of Constantinople, therefore, mainly means to analyse the sources where they are mentioned or, in the best case, described. Works of 'serious' high-level literature with statues as their subject are, however, very rare; the most notable of these are the description of the statues in the Zeuxippos bath by Christodoros of Koptos from the sixth century, and in *On the Statues* by Niketas Choniates, in which he describes the artworks destroyed by the Crusaders in 1204.

Most information about the statues of Constantinople is contained in two literary works of a more popular character, the so-called *Parastaseis syntomoi chronikai* and the *Patria* of Constantinople.

The *Parastaseis syntomoi chronikai* is a collection of eighty-nine entries of widely varying length about the statues of Constantinople which has come

---

[1] See Mango, 'Antique statuary'; Dagron, *Constantinople imaginaire*, pp. 127–59; Bassett, *Urban Image*.

[2] See Section 18 below.

[3] *LSA*-8 (Lenaghan), 375 (Lenaghan), 1033 (Gehn), 1040 (Gehn), 1160 (Gehn),1167 (Gehn), 1168 (Gehn), 2416–8 (Gehn), in the *Last Statues of Antiquity (LSA)* database, http://laststatues .classics.ox.ac.uk; see Gehn and Ward-Perkins, 'Constantinople'. Judging from the places of discovery, *LSA*-1167 and 1168 may have belonged to the decoration of the Chalke, the monumental entrance gate of the Great Palace, and *LSA*-1040 to the Capitol. On the Capitol, see Section 9 below.

down to us in one manuscript, the Paris. gr. 1336 from the eleventh century.[4] Its text is often corrupted and sometimes difficult to understand.[5] The title means 'short historical remarks' and actually refers only to the first part of it, not to the whole text.[6] The main part of it was apparently collected by several anonymous authors in the eighth century, beginning shortly after the second reign of Justinian II (705–11).[7] Recently, it has been argued that the *Parastaseis* represent the endeavour of a group of bureaucrats from old Constantinopolitan families who claimed that they alone were able to understand the real meaning of the statues in the city, thus forming a sort of xenophobic opposition to arrivistes in the imperial service.[8]

The *Parastaseis* have a very peculiar view on the city and its monuments. A particular oddity is, for example, its complete indifference towards Emperor Justinian I and his age: neither the Nika Riots in 532, which caused massive destruction in the city centre, nor the following rebuilding receive any mention.

When dealing with the ancient statues of Constantinople, the *Parastaseis* do not aim at a detailed and objective description but try to connect these statues to the local history of Byzantium by identifying them either with historical persons or by reading them as predictions of the future. The statues, which were often larger than life and either dressed in an antiquated way or even nude, are perceived as menacing and demonic. The ancient Greek religion was associated with magic practices, and as a result many statues were regarded as enchanted. It was believed that some of them transported apocalyptic prophecies about the end of Constantinople and the world, that they were animated by sorcery and maliciously took action against the people,[9] or that they were set up by ancient philosophers or magicians as talismans to protect the city from evil.

An example of an animated, evil statue can be found in a story of the *Parastaseis* about the Kynegion, an old amphitheatre on the acropolis of Byzantium.[10] A group of intellectuals visits the place and discusses the statues standing there. When one of these statues is addressed wrongly by a certain Himerios, it falls from its height and kills him. The statue is then buried on the

---

[4] For a scan, see https://gallica.bnf.fr/ark:/12148/btv1b10722877z, from fol. 111.

[5] The passages quoted below follow the translation by Cameron and Herrin, *Constantinople*, but are corrected or adapted where necessary.

[6] See Odorico, 'Du recueil à l'invention du texte'.

[7] Some entries, which are not relevant in our context, show that additions were still being made in the early ninth century or even later; see Cameron and Herrin, *Constantinople*, p. 27; and Berger, *Untersuchungen*, pp. 41–8, 674f.

[8] Anderson, 'Classified knowledge'.

[9] James, 'Pray not to fall into temptation'; Jouette, 'Divination'; Chatterjee, 'Viewing the unknown'.

[10] *Parastaseis*, c. 28.

order of Emperor Philippikos (711–3), and the first-person narrator Theodoros ends his report with these words:

> Consider these things truly, Philokalos, and pray not to fall into temptation, and take care when you look at old statues, especially pagan ones.

The idea of ancient statues acting as talismans for the city appears first in the sixth-century Chronicle of Ioannes Malalas, who claims that the well-known philosopher Apollonios of Tyana, who lived in the age of Nero (54–68), installed such talismans in Byzantium:[11]

> On entering the town of Byzas, which is now felicitously known as Constantinople, he made many talismans there too at the request of the Byzantines, one for the storks, one for the river Lykos which runs through the middle of the city, one for the tortoise, one for horses, as well as other miraculous things.

Apollonios never, as far as we know, set foot in Byzantium, but some of these statues are, without reference to him as a person, also mentioned by later sources.[12] In Malalas' chronicle, the story of the talismans is just one paragraph; the *Parastaseis*, by contrast, is a whole literary work devoted to the statues of Constantinople and often mentions their magical powers.

Talismans were also sometimes destroyed by bad or ignorant persons, or a person was punished for removing an enchanted statue, such as the eunuch Platon whose deed was, in turn, remembered by a statue near the Church of the Tortoise.[13]

Ancient statues were also occasionally used for practices of sympathetic magic, that is, for magic by which a person is connected to a statue and then suffers whatever is done to this object. This belief does not yet appear in the *Parastaseis*, but in several later texts about the statues of Constantinople.[14]

The Byzantine text commonly known today as *Patria Konstantinoupoleos* was compiled in the late tenth century, mostly of older material from the sixth to ninth centuries. The word *Patria* (neuter plural) means the local history of a place and therefore fits in content only to the first book, but is also used today for the second and third book. Book II, originally titled *About Statues*,

[11] Ioannes Malalas, 10.51; the storks also in Hesychios, c. 25. The portrait bust of marble *LSA*-375, which was found in Constantinople, could well represent Apollonios. See also Mango, 'Antique statuary'; and Section 17.6 below. On the concept of talismans in general, see Griebeler, 'Serpent Column', pp. 91–4.

[12] For the river god, see under Section 10 below.

[13] *Parastaseis*, c. 26; for the church, see under Section 11 below.

[14] See the stories about the 'Hungarian woman' in 1167, the figure under the hoof of the horse at the Tauros, and the three-headed statue in the Hippodrome, below Sections 6, 8 and 12; cf. Mango, 'Antique statuary', p. 61.

consists of 110 entries, of which more than half are taken from the *Parastaseis* – partly from a tradition that is very close to the surviving manuscript, and partly via an intermediate source, which also exists today as an independent text. In both cases, passages of the text which are difficult to understand have been smoothed and often greatly reduced.

Another important source for the monuments and statues of Constantinople are the works of Constantine of Rhodes, a well-known poet in the first half of the tenth century who was also probably one of the compilers of the Greek Anthology.[15] Only a part of his poems on Constantinople have survived in their original shape, in the description of the seven wonders of Constantinople, which now serves as the introduction to his *ekphrasis* (description) of the Church of the Apostles.[16] In the late eleventh century, the chronicle of Georgios Kedrenos quotes these poems in a list of monuments of Constantinople that is placed at the end of the reign of Theodosios I (379–95). But these quotations come apparently from a more complete version of the text, and complete or fragmentary verses at many other places indicate that Kedrenos had additional poems by the same author at his disposal, which are now lost.[17]

Before we begin our discussion in more detail, a general remark about the terminology of 'statues' is also necessary: the words mostly used by the sources for representations of persons are *agalma* or *stele*. While *agalma* mostly refers to a free-standing statue in the modern sense, *stele* may mean either a statue, a relief or even a mosaic or fresco, and the context often does not allow us to distinguish them clearly.[18] *Andrias* would clearly mean a statue, but is, for example, only once used in the *Parastaseis* and never in the *Patria*.[19] The following example may demonstrate where the problem of terminology lies. The *Parastaseis* state in Chapter 34:

> Beyond the Chalke at the Milion to the east are Constantine and Helena above the arch. There, too, a cross of the city <and the Tyche> in the middle of the cross.

The words 'and the Tyche' have been erased, but can be restored from the secondary tradition. In *Patria* 2.29 this has become:

---

[15] Cameron, *Greek Anthology*, pp. 300–7.   [16] Constantine of Rhodes.

[17] Georgios Kedrenos; see, for example, Mango et al., 'Palace of Lausus'. Mango, ibid., p. 92, listed eleven full and three half verses, to which at least another eight full and eight half verses can be added.

[18] On the terminology of statues in ancient Greece, see Keesling, 'Greek statue terms'.

[19] The term is applied in the *Parastaseis*, as in many other texts, to the statue of Paneas; the story of the bleeding woman comes originally from Eusebios (see n. 23 below), where the word *andrias* is not used.

Statues of Constantine and Helena are on the arch of the Milion. They hold a cross that can also be seen there to the east, and the Tyche of the city is in the middle of the cross, a small chain which is locked and enchanted. It ensures that no commodity of any kind is lacking, and brings all victory over the pagans, so that they are unable to approach, to get inside or to come again and again, but stay far away and return home in defeat. The chain's key was buried at the bases of the columns.

The iconography of Constantine and Helena holding the cross between them appears in Byzantium only in the ninth century when the production of free-standing sculptures had long ended. We should assume therefore that this representation, if it existed at all, was a relief, not a monumental group of statues as often shown on popular reconstructions. The Tyche, the semi-pagan town goddess of Constantinople, is usually depicted with a mural crown, a cornucopia and one foot on a ship's bow. If she was actually depicted in the middle of a cross, the picture must have been a relief medallion – but the *Patria* change this to a completely different concept in which the fortune of the city is secured by a magical device.

The foundation of Constantinople in November 324 and its earliest phase before and after the inauguration on the 11th May 330 is only briefly documented by contemporary texts. The earliest remarks about statues in the city can be found in Eusebios' *Life of Constantine* who says:[20]

> He displayed the sacred bronze figures, of which the error of the ancients had for a long time been proud, to all the public in all the squares of the Emperor's city, so that in one place the Pythian was displayed as a contemptible spectacle to the viewers, in another the Sminthian, in the Hippodrome itself the tripods from Delphi, and the Muses of Helicon at the palace.

The Pythian and Sminthian Apollo mentioned here cannot be identified with statues which existed later in the city. The Muses were a group of nine statues which had been brought from the famous sanctuary on Mount Helikon – several rhetorical texts from the fourth century allude to their presence by calling Constantinople 'the new seat of the Muses'. But these statues were destroyed in 403 when the first Hagia Sophia and the nearby building of the Senate, where they had stood, burned down. Zosimos, the last pagan historian, who wrote about eighty years later, insists that two other ancient statues, a Zeus from Dodone and an Athena from Lindos, survived the fire miraculously.[21] But let us go on with Eusebios' report:

---

[20] Eusebios, *Life of Constantine*, ch. 3.54.2–3; on which see Bassett, 'Curious art', pp. 246–7.
[21] Zosimos, 5.24.3–8.

> The city named after the Emperor was filled throughout with objects of
> skilled artwork in bronze dedicated in various provinces. To these under the
> name of gods those sick with error had for long ages vainly offered innumer-
> able hecatombs and whole burnt sacrifices, but now they at last learnt sense,
> as the Emperor used these very toys for the laughter and amusement of the
> spectators.

Constantine the Great is depicted as a purely Christian emperor whose aim was
to destroy all remnants of paganism – but, as we shall see presently, this was
definitely not the case, and many ancient statues brought to Constantinople in
his era were intended for a pagan or semi-pagan religious context, beginning
with the main monument of the new city: the emperor's own statue on the
column of his new forum.

Following a similar ideological representation, Eusebios speaks also some
chapters before about 'Daniel with his lions shaped in bronze and glinting with
gold leaf'.[22] It is highly improbable, however, that such a Christian group of
statues ever existed; we should rather assume that this was a reinterpreted
ancient work of art, like the group of Christ and the bleeding woman of
Paneas in Palestine which is also mentioned in Eusebios' work.[23]

Only about fifty years after the foundation of Constantinople, Jerome mentions the transport of many ancient statues to Constantinople in his chronicle
Constantinopolis dedicatur omnium paene urbium nuditate. This is usually
translated as 'Constantinople was dedicated by denudating almost all cities',
but may also mean 'by the nudities of almost all cities'.[24]

Later texts of the post-iconoclastic time show a strong tendency to date all
buildings and objects in the city, which were obviously from the early Byzantine
period, back to Constantine, its founder and first Christian emperor, or in the
best case even to the time before him. In reality it took a long time to build the
city and to bring it into an inhabitable shape: by 330, it seems, only the walls and
some important public buildings were actually completed; for example, the
Forum of Constantine immediately outside the old walls of Byzantium and the
Capitol further to the west. For most of the area now incorporated into the city,
only plans had been made, and it was over the course of some decades that it
became filled with streets and squares, houses and public buildings. The
aqueduct, which was indispensable for the water supply of the growing population, was put into service only in 373, and the Fora of Theodosios and Arkadios
on the main east–west avenue, the so-called Mese, were completed and inaugurated only in 393 and in 421 respectively.

---

[22] Eusebios, *Life of Constantine*, ch. 3.48.   [23] Eusebios, *Church History*, 7.18.
[24] Martins de Jesus, 'Nude Constantinople', p. 1.

All this suggests that the ancient statues which decorated Constantinople were not all brought to the city at the same time, or let's say the six years between 324 and 330, but in the course of several decades. A part of them, however, was apparently set up with a clear political agenda – namely, that of the semi-pagan imperial cult of Constantine himself. And, as it seems, a number of statues were actually transferred to Constantinople as a kind of basic equipment for this purpose before the city had even been inaugurated.

The complete Christianisation of the empire and its heavy political decline during the seventh century interrupted the traditions of ancient culture and religion almost completely, especially among the uneducated population. The real significance of Constantinople's ancient statues was no longer understood, and new identifications were proposed for the historical and mythological persons depicted by them, as well as for the pagan deities. Statues of ancient kings and other rulers were sometimes identified with emperors of Constantinople's Byzantine past, while the iconography of ancient gods and goddesses precluded, in most cases, their interpretation as biblical or Christian persons. The commonest reinterpretation of ancient statues is, therefore, that of the *Parastaseis*: as magical figures set up by ancient philosophers or sorcerers, with the intention either to do harm to the city, or to keep harm away from it.

The following pages will not try to give a list of the many statues of emperors and dignitaries which stood in public buildings or on the streets of Constantinople. Instead, I will present the important pieces of which we know, with a special focus on their arrangement in groups and their popular reception. After a look on the imperial statues on triumphal columns, I will first follow the main street, the *Mese*, from the city centre to the west. Then, returning to the centre, I will visit the collections of statues on the Augoustaion square, in the Zeuxippos baths, in the Lausos Palace, and, above all, in the Hippodrome.

2 'Shining like the Sun upon the Citizens': Constantine's Statue on the Forum

The first monument of Constantinople was a triumphal column with the statue of Constantine the Great on top. It stood in the centre of his newly built circular forum, immediately outside the main gate of old Byzantium, and was inaugurated together with the city on the 11th May 330.

Until the early seventh century, at least another six triumphal columns were built in Constantinople, all crowned by the statue of an emperor. But only the column of Constantine and another smaller column have survived to our day, and most statues, that of Constantine included, were lost in the Byzantine age.

The statue of Emperor Justinian was the last to go, still standing on its column near Hagia Sophia when Constantinople was taken by the Ottomans in 1453, and another statue, the so-called Colossus of Barletta, has survived outside the city.[25]

The column of Constantine with its height of almost 40 metres and the gilded, brightly shining statue on top was certainly the most impressive monument of the new city in its first decades. In the so-called *Tabula Peutingeriana*, a Roman road map from the fourth century which survives in a late medieval copy, a picture of it symbolises Constantinople, together with the enthroned city goddess. This representation is small and not very detailed, but the only one which was drawn while the statue still existed.

No source before the mid-sixth century mentions the statue as such or describes it in any detail, and only the *Parastaseis* tell us, more than four hundred years after the event, how it was installed on the column in 330: it was placed on a carriage, escorted to the new forum, and lifted to the top of the column in the presence of the whole population, and revered as embodying the Tyche of the city. The first descriptions of the statue can be found in the works of Hesychios of Miletus and of John Malalas, which were both written in the mid-sixth century – more than two hundred years after Constantine. Hesychios speaks of 'the notable porphyry column, on which Constantine is set, whom we see shining like the sun upon the citizens',[26] while Malalas states that he 'put a statue of himself on top of this same column, which had seven rays on its head. He brought this work of bronze which had stood in Ilion, a town of Phrygia'.[27]

The claim that the statue was a reused piece of ancient Greek art can only be explained if the statue did not show the emperor in the usual military costume, but in a way which suggested identification as a pagan god. The most plausible assumption is that the statue was, in fact, reused, that it was naked, as the picture in the *Tabula Peutingeriana* suggests, and that it wore a crown with seven solar rays emanating from its head in an angle.[28]

The depiction of a Roman emperor in this form is not without precedent, the most prominent example being the monumental Colossus of Nero in Rome which was naked, had such a radiate crown and was rededicated after his death to the Sun. In the case of Constantine, the iconography can be explained by his association with the cult of Sol Invictus, the invincible sun god, which lasted from 310 to 325. In this period, Sol appeared regularly on the emperor's coins. Sol was also propagated as his supporter in the victory over Maxentius in 312 and figures prominently on the Arch of Constantine, which was built in Rome to commemorate this event.

---

[25] See Section 3 below.   [26] Hesychios, c. 45.   [27] Ioannes Malalas, 13.7.
[28] Bardill, *Constantine*, pp. 27–34.

Figure 1 The column of Constantine in the *Tabula Peutingeriana*.
Credit: Vienna, Austrian National Library, Cod. 324.

Since it is improbable that a statue of this size or shape was newly made for the column of Constantine's city, we should assume that a colossal statue of a Hellenistic king or a god was actually reused here. But there is no reason to believe Malalas that it came from Ilion, the Roman successor settlement of Troy, for this claim is simply an allusion to the legend that Constantine transferred the legitimate title to world rule, that of the Trojans, from Rome back to the East.[29] The statue may rather have been, as suggested by Jonathan Bardill, that of the Greek sun god Helios, which stood in older times, according to Malalas, on a public square of Byzantium and was later transferred to a new temple of Helios on the acropolis.[30] The attribution of this temple to Septimius Severus (193–211) is, however, certainly wrong, for Severus destroyed the walls of Byzantium and deprived the city of its rights, but did not rebuild it – as the later legend claimed.[31]

The central monument of Constantinople was, therefore, clearly and visibly pagan in character. After Constantine's death in 337, the city soon

---

[29] Bardill, *Constantine*, p. 34, with note 19.   [30] Ibid.; Ioannes Malalas, 12.20.
[31] See Section 4 below; and Mango, 'Septime Severe'.

became Christian, and Constantine himself was perceived as the first Christian emperor, and later even venerated as a saint. But the naked statue in the shape of the sun god still stood on its column, and the longer it stood there, the more it became incomprehensible to its beholders. The forum was experienced as a pagan place – also on account of the other ancient statues which stood there – a fact which began to cause troubles for the regular ecclesiastical processions which passed through it. We hear that the globe fell down in 477 and was repaired, and the same happened to the spear in 557.[32] When the globe fell for the second time at the earthquake of 869, it was put in its place again, but at the same occasion a chapel of the Mother of God was built at the foot of the column. In this way, the forum was Christianised, and the processions visited the chapel on several occasions, now probably without even taking a look at the statue.[33]

Hesychios' remark 'whom we see shining like the sun upon the citizens' indicates that the statue was originally gilded. In later sources, such as the tenth-century Chronicle of the Logothete, this phrase is turned into an inscription in verse, 'To Constantine who shines upon the citizens like the sun' – which cannot have, however, stood on the socle, since in Constantine's age it would have been in Latin and in hexameters, while this inscription is in Byzantine dodecasyllables, a meter which was used in Byzantine epigrammatic poetry only from the seventh century onwards.[34]

The *Patria*, in the late tenth century, are the first to call the statue *Anelios*, that is, 'Un-Sun'.[35] This is probably a pun on the old designation as *Anthelios* or 'Anti-Sun',[36] in the sense of 'second sun' or 'competing sun', thus indicating that the gilding was now lost. In 1079, the *Anelios* and parts of the column were damaged by lightning, as Michael Attaleiates reports.[37] Finally, on the 5th April 1106, the statue fell down during a thunderstorm killing several people, and was later replaced by a cross.[38] In her report on this event, the historian Anna Komnene writes that the statue had looked to the east with a sceptre in the right hand and a globe in the left. The statue, she says, was one of Apollo which Constantine had renamed after himself, and was called *Anelios* by the inhabitants of Constantinople. The fact that Anna speaks about a sceptre may indicate that the original spear had been replaced

[32] Theophanes, p. 126.2, 222.25–30.
[33] Symeon Logothetes, c. 101.8; see Mango, 'Constantine's porphyry column'.
[34] Κωνσταντίνῳ λάμποντι ἡλίου δίκην: Symeon Logothetes, c. 88.7. The same applies for the Christian inscription quoted by Constantine of Rhodes, v. 67–74, and repeated in Georgios Kedrenos, c. 344.8.
[35] *Patria*, 2.49.   [36] Mentioned by Anna Komnene, see n. 38 below.
[37] Michael Attaleiates, p. 309; also Michael Glykas, p. 617.
[38] Anna Komnene, 12.4.5; Ioannes Zonaras, vol. 3, p. 755.6–14.

Figure 2 Constantine's statue on the column of his forum.
Credit: Reconstruction by Tayfun Öner.

by a sceptre during an undocumented restoration, perhaps by a labaron, that is, a military standard with a flag fixed at a horizontal bar, and bearing the monogram of Christ.

By the time of its destruction the statue had become, in the general perception, a purely pagan object whose relationship to the great Christian emperor Constantine was difficult to understand. Anna reports that, when the statue had fallen, some people took this as a bad omen for the impending death of the emperor, Alexios I Komnenos. But when the emperor was informed about these rumours, he said: 'I know one lord of life and death, and there is no reason why I should believe that the fall of pagan statues brings death.'

3 Other Statues of Emperors on Triumphal Columns

In the decades after Constantine's death, Constantinople changed its character from a semi-pagan place of his imperial cult to a new, Christian Rome and capital of the East. In the age of Theodosios I (379–95), the pagan temples in the city were closed and churches built instead, and monuments of his own dynasty, competing with those of Constantine the Great, were erected in the new parts of the city.

The place chosen by Theodosios to immortalise his memory was his new forum, which lay about 700 metres west of that of Constantine in the present region of Bayezid. It featured a triumphal column, a nymphaeum and a basilica, i.e., a courtroom and town hall. The forum was usually not called by the emperor's name but rather Tauros or 'bull', for a reason that is unknown. Parts of the arch at its western entrance, which must have had a pendant on the eastern side, and the foundations of the surrounding walls have been excavated.[39] They show that its size has been greatly overestimated – for it did not measure more than about 55 × 55 m – and that the column with the statue of Theodosios I on top stood in the middle of it.[40]

The column was completed in 386, and the statue set up in 393.[41] In contrast to the statue in the Forum of Constantine the Great, it was probably newly made and had the same iconographical type as that which can be seen today in the still existing statue of Leon I (457–74), showing the emperor in military costume. [42] The statue of Theodosios formed an ensemble with two equestrian statues on the ground, which represented his sons Arkadios and Honorios. They both survived for a long time, developing their own legends, and will be discussed later in this section and in Section 8.

In 480 the statue was destroyed by an earthquake. In 506 an official called John the Paphlagonian gave an order to melt down a number of bronze statues that had allegedly been brought to the city by Constantine the Great, and to cast a big new statue of Emperor Anastasios, which was then placed on the empty column.[43] But only six years later, in 512, this statue was destroyed during a popular uprising. From that time, the column was empty again, but still much admired for its decoration with a spiral relief; it was finally destroyed in the early Ottoman age.[44]

The next imperial forum to the west was that of Arkadios (395–408) on the so-called Xerolophos, or 'dry hill'. Since the column with the emperor's statue

---

[39] Naumann, 'Neue Beobachtungen'.   [40] Berger, 'Tauros e Sigma', pp. 7–24.

[41] Theophanes, p. 70.20–1; *Chronicon paschale*, p. 565.6–8.   [42] See below.

[43] Ioannes Malalas, 16.13.

[44] Marcellinus comes, pp. 92.8–9, 96.31–2, 98.5; Theophanes, p. 126.2–3 with date 477.

was set up only in 421, it seems that the forum was planned by Arkadios, but built only after his death in his honour. The statue, which was probably similar to that of Theodosios, fell down in 740.[45] Only the column itself and perhaps some statues on ground level survived for a long time. The column was finally dismantled in 1716, and only its sockle now remains.[46]

The son of Arkadios, Theodosios II, came to the throne as a child and reigned for a long time (408–50); it is strange that apparently no monumental column was built for him. Only the *Patria* mention his statue on a column at the Sigma, allegedly erected by the eunuch and chamberlain Chrysaphios.[47] The Sigma, a semicircular courtyard, was the only remaining part of the Palace of Helena (positioned outside the Constantinian walls on the main street).[48]

The successor of Theodosios II, Emperor Markianos (450–7), was remembered by a column which still stands today and has this Latin inscription on its sockle: PRINCIPIS HANC STATUAM MARCIANI CERNE FORUMQUE / PRAEFECTUS VOVIT QUOD TATIANUS OPUS ('See this statue of Marcian and his forum, a work which the prefect Tatianus has dedicated'). Although the column, which stands on the northern branch of the main street leading to the Church of the Holy Apostles, is rather modest in size, it is still strange that no Byzantine source mentions it, and that no European had ever seen it before the French traveller Pierre Gilles in the mid-sixteenth century.[49] The explanation can probably be found in the tenth-century *Book of Ceremonies:* when describing imperial processions to the Church of the Apostles, it lists the places where receptions took place on the way, among them being 'the lions' at exactly the place we should expect to find the column of Markianos.[50] This suggests that the statue had already disappeared by that time, and that two statues of lions at the foot of the column had become the main objects of interest of this small forum.

A much more prominent column was erected for Emperor Leon I (457–74) on the old acropolis of Byzantium, in front of the praetorian prefect's residence, on a square elsewhere called 'the petitions' (*pittakia*).[51] No written source mentions it except the *Parastaseis* where we read:[52]

> The so-called petition man (*pittakes*) is Leon the Great, who is called the Butcher by the many. Also the receptions of the emperors were held there, and also a palace was established near the old church of Saint Eirene, as Ioannes Diakrinomenos says.

---

[45] Marcellinus comes, p. 75.4–6; Theophanes, p. 412.10–11.   [46] Konrad, 'Beobachtungen'.
[47] *Patria*, 2.57.   [48] Berger, 'Tauros e Sigma', pp. 24–31.
[49] Gyllius, De topographia Constantinopoleos, book 4, p. 2.
[50] Constantine Porphyrogennetos, *De cerimoniis*, I, 5.64.
[51] Berger, *Untersuchungen*, pp. 394–6.   [52] *Parastaseis*, c. 67.

Figure 3 The Colossus of Barletta.
Credit: Photograph by Dmitriy Moroz, Alamy Stock Photo.

As often in this text, the name of the place has been changed to a name of the statue by adding a male ending.

The dismembered parts of a monumental column, which may once have supported Leon's statue, can still be seen in the second courtyard of the Topkapı Palace in İstanbul. Among them is a marble block with recesses on the upper side, which fit the feet of a monumental bronze statue of an emperor that was found in the sea near Barletta in southern Italy in 1309 – and subsequently set up in the city. We may assume therefore that this 'Colossus of Barletta' was part of the Venetian booty at the conquest of Constantinople in 1204, and was lost during transport to Venice.[53]

This is the only extant late-antique statue of an emperor that survives almost undamaged; only the upper part of the skull and the lower part of the legs are lost and have been replaced. The statue, which is slightly over 5 metres high, gives us a clear indication of how we are to imagine the earlier imperial statues of Constantinople: the emperor is shown in military costume, with a now lost spear or labaron in his left hand, and a globe in his right.

After Leon's death in 474, no triumphal columns were built for several decades, neither in the reign of Zenon (475–91) nor that of Justin I (518–27); only Anastasios, as mentioned above, tried to occupy the empty place on the column of Theodosios with his own statue, but without lasting success.

When Emperor Justinian I came to power in 527, a period of great political ambitions began. The so-called Nika Riots in 532, which almost cost Justinian his throne but were finally put down by military force, led to massive destruction by fire in the city centre and then its subsequent reconstruction. The new, domed Church of Hagia Sophia, which still stands today, was inaugurated in 537, and six years later, in 543, the triumphal column of the emperor was built on the Augoustaion square immediately in front of the church.[54] This column stood, with Justinian's statue on it, until the end of the empire in 1453. Shortly thereafter, the column was dismantled by the Ottomans and the statue melted down, but not before being drawn by an Italian artist.[55]

Justinian is portrayed by the statue as a rider on his horse, something which contradicts all ancient conventions for statues on high columns.[56] The reason is clearly stated in the Chronicle of Ioannes Malalas:[57]

> And in the same year an equestrian statue of the emperor Justinian was raised up near the palace on the so-called Augoustaion. This was the statue of the emperor Arkadios which had stood before on the Tauros on a sockle.

The fifteenth-century drawing of the statue shows the inscription on the horse FONS GLORIAE PERENNIS THEODOSI ('source of eternal glory of Theodosios') which supports this identification. We do not know why no new statue was made for this column and an old one reused instead, but it should also be said

---

[53] Peschlow, 'Ehrensäule'; this identification is still disputed, see Kiilerich, 'Barletta Colossus'.
[54] Mango, 'Columns'.   [55] On this drawing, see Lehmann, 'Theodosius or Justinian?'.
[56] For the column and statue, see in detail Boeck, *Bronze Horseman*.
[57] Ioannes Malalas, 18.94.

Figure 4 The statue of Justinian on the Augoustaion.

Credit: Budapest, University Library and Archives of Eötvös Loránd University, Cod. Ital. 3, fol. 144 v.

that the column was constructed in a rather unconventional way of brick without an inner staircase, and revetted with gilded bronze slabs.

The riding emperor is portrayed in the drawing in triumphal dress with a *toupha* on his head, i.e., a plumed helmet with peacock feathers; he holds a globe in his left hand and stretches his right hand to the east.

Justinian's rider was the only monumental bronze statue in Constantinople which survived the destructions in 1204, and only one such monument was erected after the reconquest in 1261 – the column of Michael VIII, which could probably not be compared to it in size and importance.

In the last centuries of Byzantium, Justinian's statue became a symbol of the city and the state, just as the statue of Constantine had been in the early days of

Constantinople. The formation of legends, however, had begun already in Justinian's own time. Prokopios of Kaisareia, for example, his contemporary and court historian, describes the statue in great detail and ends with these words:[58]

> He looks toward the rising sun, directing his course, I suppose, against the Persians. And in his left hand he holds a globe, by which the sculptor signifies that the whole earth and sea are subject to him, yet he has neither sword nor spear nor any other weapon, but a cross stands upon the globe which he carries, the emblem by which alone he has obtained both his empire and his victory in war. And stretching forth his right hand toward the rising sun and spreading out his fingers, he commands the barbarians in that region to remain at home and to advance no further. So much, then, for this.

In the *Patria*, which are based at this point on Prokopios' account, we read:[59]

> He holds in his left hand a globe which has a cross fixed on it and means that he had become lord of all the earth because of his faith in the cross – for the earth is a globe because of its spherical shape, and the cross is faith because God was nailed to it in the flesh. He has his right hand extended to the East, giving the Persians a sign that they should stop and not advance into Roman territory, saying, by raising and warding off with his hand: 'Stop, Persians, and do not go further, for this will be of no benefit for you.'

This perception of the statue is still attested in the last years of Byzantium, now with the Turks replacing the Persians. The globe or 'golden apple' in the rider's hand, as the late sources call it, finally became the symbol of the city's fortune – it seems, in fact, that it fell down more than once and was fixed again for this very reason.[60] Referring to the globe, the Turks called Constantinople as a whole the 'golden apple', and later used this name for their next objects of desire, such as Belgrade and Vienna. Some Russian icons down to the seventeenth century show, as part of an architectural background, a statue on horseback on a column and next to a church.[61]

By the time Justinian died in 565, the crisis of the empire had already begun. The last triumphal column was erected by his nephew and successor Justin II (565–78) at the Deuteron, a place on the northwestern main avenue

---

[58] Prokopios, *Buildings*, 1.2.10–12.   [59] *Patria*, 2.17.
[60] Van der Vin, *Travellers*, vol. 1, p. 275: the globe fell down in 1316, was restored in 1325, had fallen again by 1427, and a last attempt was made in 1430–5 to fix it again.
[61] Belobrova, 'Статуя'.

Figure 5 Constantinople in the fifteenth century.
Credit: Bodleian Library, Ms. Canon. Misc. 378, fol. 84r.[62]

beyond the Church of the Apostles. The statue fell down at the earthquake of 866, while the column was dismantled only in the sixteenth century.[63]

After that time and down to the end of the empire in the fifteenth century, no further columns of monumental dimension were built in Constantinople. We hear that in 596, under Emperor Mauricius, a terrace was constructed near the Magnaura, an audience hall in the northeast of the Great Palace, and his statue

---

[62] See Boeck, *Imagining*, p. 244. A similar picture can be found in the Codex Matritensis Reserva 36, fol. 84r.

[63] Berger, *Untersuchungen*, pp. 518–20; for its destruction, see Gyllius, *De topographia Constantinopoleos*, book 1, p. 14, and book 4, p. 1.

set up there.[64] Since the *Parastaseis* tell us that Emperor Phokas, who had overthrown Mauricius in 602, had his statue set up in the same area shortly before his downfall in 610,[65] we may assume that his statue replaced that of Mauricius. No word is said about a column at this place, but the *Patria* add to their excerpt from the *Parastaseis* that the statue of Phokas had been placed on a column of masonry.[66]

The last imperial column was also erected by the same Phokas in the year 609. It stood on a courtyard on top of a cistern, and must therefore have been of rather modest dimensions. When Herakleios came to power in 610, instead of a statue a cross was put on top of this column in 612. At an unknown time in the reign of the same emperor, but probably before 626, a gilded statue of the emperor's cousin, the patrician Niketas, was set up on a four-column monument in the Forum of Constantine.[67] If this information is correct, this was the last statue, though probably a reused one, which was set up in the city for many centuries.

The production of hollow-cast bronze statues had already ended by this time and was never resumed in the Byzantine age. When two emperors attempted, many centuries later, to set up bronze statues in their own honour, they must have appropriated old works of art for this purpose.

The first case is that of Andronikos I Komnenos (1183–5) who renovated, according to the historian Niketas Choniates, the Church of the Forty Martyrs as his own foundation and burial site, and planned to set up a statue of bronze on a column near the Anemodoulion nearby but was overthrown and killed before this could take place.

A second, more successful case is that of Michael VIII Palaiologos (1259–82)[68] who let a column be built near the Church of the Apostles, on which his statue was installed, kneeling before the archangel Michael. This group was probably put together from two reused and perhaps moderately reworked ancient pieces, namely the kneeling figure of a barbarian offering gifts and a winged victory. The column was destroyed in 1296 by an earthquake and restored. Russian and western visitors of the late Byzantine period identified the kneeling emperor not with Michael VIII Palaiologos but with Constantine the Great.

4 Of Emperors and Elephants

Let us now begin our promenade along the main avenue of Constantinople, the Mese, from the city centre to the Golden Gate in the west, and have a look on the statues that stood at various locations along this avenue. Our starting point will

---

[64] Theophanes, p. 274.22–4.   [65] *Parastaseis*, c. 74.   [66] *Patria*, 2.34.
[67] Nikephoros, *Breviarium*, c. 5; Mango, 'Epigrammes', pp. 30–1, and 'Columns', pp. 14–17. Two dedicatory epigrams for this statue are preserved as *Anthologia graeca*, 16.46 and 16.47.
[68] Thomov, 'Last column'.

be the Basilica with the Milion, the Golden Milestone, in front of it; the basic textual sources will be the *Parastaseis*, with supplements from other texts such as the *Patria*.

The *Parastaseis* contain a list of seven attractions or 'spectacles', most of which can be located on the Mese. The first of them is the Basilica:[69]

> Spectacle number one. – The gilt statue of a man in the golden-roofed Basilica colonnade, where the measure of the emperor Herakleios was set up, the kneeling one, is of Justinian when he was tyrant of Constantinople for the second time, and next to him is his wife, the sister of Ibouzeros Gliabanos, after the defeat of Tiberios Apsimar, when Philippikos also was censured in that part of the golden-roofed Basilica. Tervel of Bulgaria and Gliabanos the Khazar took their places there on many occasions, and so large payments of tribute were made here, at the site of the statues of the tyrant and his wife.

This part of the chapter contains some plausible information on historical events in the second reign of Justinian II (705–11) and is the only source which knows the name of the Khazar khagan Gliabanos. The identification of the kneeling statue as Justinian is, however, probably inaccurate. Statues of bronze were no longer produced in the time of Justinian II, and the humble posture alone excludes the possibility that the kneeling man was actually the portrait of an emperor. The mention of a second statue, that of his wife, suggests that the text actually conflates two objects, a kneeling man – probably a barbarian from an older imperial representation – and a standing royal couple which can perhaps be identified with the group Hesychios of Milet had, in the sixth century, interpreted as Byzas (the legendary king and founder of Byzantium) and his wife Pheidaleia. Justinian II, therefore, has in reality nothing to do with these statues. This does not deny, on the other hand, that the historical events mentioned actually took place at the Basilica.

The *Patria* mention, some two hundred years later than the *Parastaseis*, another statue of bronze (which cannot be identified with one of those described here), namely king Solomon, sitting on a throne, holding his cheek and looking at Hagia Sophia – by which Emperor Justinian has surpassed the splendour of his temple in Jerusalem.[70] Of course, this statue did not show Solomon; rather, the *Patria* allude here to the well-known legend that Justinian, when entering Hagia Sophia for the first time, shouted the words 'I have defeated you, Solomon'. Another source states that Basileios I (867–86) reworked this piece as his portrait, and then placed it in the foundations of his great New Church in the palace area.[71]

---

[69] *Parastaseis*, c. 37. [70] *Patria*, 2.40. [71] Symeon Logothetes, c. 132.14.

Let us now return to the text of the *Parastaseis* whose next section describes the statue of an elephant that stood there, set in an entirely mythical context:

> With these stands a huge elephant; as the exhibitors of animals have assured us, elephants do not come greater in size than this, the big ones being as big as this. The elephant was set up by Severus the son of Carus the pagan as a spectacle, according to tradition. For in the same golden-roofed Basilica they say that the elephant lived, an extraordinary spectacle. They say that an enclosure was in front of the area of the seventy-two steps, and there was also a large force of guards there. And they say that in the same place as the elephant lived Carcinelus, a silversmith who used rigged scales. They say he threatened the elephant's keeper because his house was being damaged, and he frequently vowed that he would kill the keeper if he did not keep the animal in check. But <the keeper> refused to keep it in check because of the oil-bearing ... So <the user of rigged scales> killed him and offered him to the elephant as fodder, but the animal, being wild, killed him too. And when Severus heard this he offered many sacrifices to the beast, and they were at once commemorated in statues in that place.

In 196, Emperor Septimius Severus (195–211) destroyed the city of Byzantium because it had supported his opponent Niger in the preceding civil war, and deprived it of its municipal privileges. The Byzantine tradition, however, depicts Severus as a heroic figure, claiming that he regretted his actions and rebuilt the city, thus becoming the second founder of Byzantium after Byzas (to be followed by the third and final founder, Constantine the Great).[72] As a result, the foundation of the Hippodrome and the nearby Zeuxippos baths is ascribed to him. But sources other than the *Parastaseis* do not mention the Basilica among his works.

A statue of an elephant must actually have stood in the Basilica, as an anecdote in the *Patria* suggests; it speaks about an elephant from India which was brought to Constantinople under Theodosios I (379–95) and kept near the Milion – the big four-sided arch in front of the Basilica – and which recognised and killed a man who had hit it with a rod ten years earlier.[73]

The Milion is the subject of the following chapter of the *Parastaseis*. The only real topographical information here is the seventy-two steps that must have led from the Basilica down to a lower terrace on which the Chalkoprateia church was built in the mid-fifth century.[74] The third section of this chapter is as follows:

> There too Herakles was worshipped, the recipient of many sacrifices. And the statue was removed to the Hippodrome to be a great spectacle. But originally it was brought from Rome to Byzantium in the time of Julian the *consularis* with a chariot and a boat and twelve statues.

---

[72] Dagron, *Naissance*, pp. 13–19. [73] *Patria*, 3.89. [74] Berger, *Untersuchungen*, pp. 419–22.

The monumental statue of Herakles is an object well known from ancient sources; it was a work of the famous sculptor Lysippos for Tarent and brought to Rome as a trophy in 209 BC. In Constantinople, it stood in the Hippodrome for many centuries and is mentioned several times as located there.[75] Only the *Parastaseis* claim that it stood first at the Milion, and that it was brought there in the time of Julian the *consularis*. If the identification of this person with the city prefect of Rome from 326 to 329 is correct,[76] the remark of the *Parastaseis* means that the statue arrived at Constantinople even before the city was officially inaugurated in 330, and therefore was part of its initial decoration.

The twelve statues which came from Rome together with Herakles are probably the Zodiac group which is mentioned later in the Hippodrome.[77] The chapter then ends with these words:

> This strange tale of the spectacle of Severus took place, they say, in the consulship of Anthimos; he was the owner of Ta Anthimou, which was traded by the order of Nouzametos the prefect, the Persian, in the place of tribute payment, in the days of Byzas and Antes. And this spectacle is accessible until the present day for philosophers to test.

This passage refers again, as the mention of Severus suggests, to the statue of the elephant; therefore, the mention of the statue of Herakles, referred to above, is a later addition to the text. A consul called Anthimos is unknown, but has been identified either with Anthemios, Praetorian prefect and consul in the East in 405, or with his homonymous grandson, consul in 455 and from 467 to 472 emperor of the West. In any case, the following passage completely leaves historical reality by dating the prefect Nouzametos into the 'days of Byzas and Antes', that is, of the two founding fathers on whom see below in Section 5. A prefect called Nouzametos is unknown, and no explanation for his name has been found so far.

5 Constantine Helios as Charioteer

One of the few statues once displayed in Constantinople that have survived until today outside the city is the group of four bronze horses now on the facade of the Church of San Marco in Venice. They are usually dated to the Hellenistic age; they bear bridles which show that they were once harnessed to a chariot, thus forming part of a quadriga, and have remains of a gilding. The *Parastaseis* describe it as their second 'spectacle':[78]

---

[75] See below, Section 17.4.   [76] Cameron and Herrin, *Constantinople*, p. 214.
[77] See below, Section 17.4.   [78] *Parastaseis*, c. 38; for another mention see Section 17.5 below.

Spectacle two, at the golden Milion. – At the golden Milion a chariot of Zeus Helios with four fiery horses, raised by two pillars, have been standing since ancient times. There Constantine the Great was acclaimed after defeating Azotios and Byzas and Antes the blue faction shouting 'You have taken up the whip again, and as though young again you race madly in the stadium'; but the Green faction said: 'We don't need you, miserable wretch; the gods above have taken him.'

The Milion is the Golden Milestone in the city centre near the Basilica and the Hippodrome; the *Patria*, however, later mention the horses inside the Hippodrome above the starting boxes.[79]

The *Parastaseis* do their best to envelop Constantinople in a cloud of a mysterious, fictional history. One way to achieve this is to date an event to 'the days of Byzas and Antes'. Byzas is the legendary founder of Byzantium in the seventh century BC and well known from other sources, while the name Antes is simply derived from the second part of the word *Byz-antion*.[80]

In this chapter, Constantine himself becomes a mythological figure and is described as fighting in person against Byzas and Antes. And after his victory, he is acclaimed by the blue circus faction – but this is done with words from an epigram in praise of the famous sixth-century charioteer Porphyrios, which was inscribed on the base of one of his monuments on the spina of the Hippodrome.[81] The epigram could be read by everyone who passed by, and whoever was able to master its archaising language must also have understood its actual meaning.[82]

The text of the *Parastaseis* then goes on:

And the chariot of Helios was brought down into the Hippodrome, and a new little statue of the *tyche* of the city was escorted in procession carried by Helios. Escorted by many officials, it came to the Stama and received prizes from the Emperor Constantine, and after being crowned, it went out and was placed in the Senate until the next birthday of the city. But because of the cross engraved on it, it was consigned by Julian to a pit where there were many other spectacles. And if anyone researches accurately the inscriptions of the Forum, he would still more be amazed.

This description of the inauguration ceremony of Constantinople has an older parallel in the Chronicle of Ioannes Malalas where, instead of the inauguration itself, rather the annual commemoration of it on the 11th May is described:[83]

[79] *Patria*, 2.75.
[80] No explanation has so far been found for the third mentioned person, Azotios, which seems to be a rendering of the Armenian royal name Ashot.
[81] *Anthologia graeca*, 15.44; cf. Cameron, *Porphyrius*, pp. 109–10. For the statues of charioteers, see also Section 17.6 below.
[82] Cameron and Herrin, *Constantinople*, p. 217.   [83] Ioannes Malalas, 13.8.

Figure 6 The horses of San Marco, Venice.
Credit: Photograph courtesy of Franz Alto Bauer.

He had another statue made of himself in gilded wood, bearing in its right hand the *tyche* of the city, itself gilded, which he called Anthousa. He ordered that on the same day as the Anniversary race-meeting this wooden statue should be brought in, escorted by the soldiers wearing cloaks and boots, all holding candles; the carriage should march around the turning post and reach the pit opposite the imperial *kathisma*, and the emperor of the time should rise and make obeisance as he gazed at this statue of Constantine and the *tyche* of the city. This custom has been maintained up to the present day.

It is clear that this ceremony must have been abolished long before Malalas' time, either by the pagan Julian (361–63), as claimed by the *Parastaseis* in the quoted entry, or by the Christian Theodosios I (379–95), as another entry of the same text says:[84]

In the Senate, charioteers were placed in their chariots and set on the astronomical instrument, where the statues of Artemis and Aphrodite stand ... The chariots were buried beneath the arch under the Emperor Theodosios.

---

[84] *Parastaseis*, c. 8.

Figure 7 The Tømmerby statuette.
Credit: Photograph courtesy of Lennart Larsen, National Museum of Denmark.

How many charioteers and chariots actually stood at the Milion and what happened to them is unknown. But at least the four horses of the main group survived, first in Constantinople and later in Venice. A bronze statuette of a charioteer with the imperial hairstyle of Constantine's age and a radiate crown, which was found in Tømmerby in Denmark, may well have belonged to a miniature copy of this group and gives us an idea how the original ensemble may have looked.[85]

If the Senate mentioned here is the place where the group was stored over the year, it must have been that at the Forum of Constantine, and will be discussed in the next section.

---

[85] Leeb, *Konstantin und Christus*, pp. 17–21; Poulsen, 'Portrait statuette'.

6 The Forum of Constantine

In addition to the statue of Constantine on his column, a number of other statues
stood on the forum on ground level. Since most of them are omitted in the report
of the *Parastaseis* about their third 'spectacle',[86] we will begin our tour of the
forum with the relevant section in the chronicle of Georgios Kedrenos. This is
an excerpt from a poem by Constantine of Rhodes where almost no information
about the history and architecture of the forum is given:[87]

> On the northern side of the Forum is the Senate which burned down under
> Leon, the husband of Verina.

A description of the gate of the Senate follows where it is said that the gate had
come from the temple of Artemis in Ephesos. The Senate at the forum was, in
fact, damaged during the great fire of 465. But since this gate with reliefs
showing a battle of the Giants is mentioned in the old Senate near the palace
in the fourth century,[88] it seems that this information has been attached here to
the wrong building, either by Constantine's source or by himself. The text then
says about the statues in front of the building:

> On the side of the Forum square stand two statues: to the west that of the
> Lindian Athene which has a helmet and the monster Gorgon and snakes
> wound around its neck, for this is how the ancients depicted her idol.

The last part of this description is missing in the poem:

> And to the east Amphitrite which has pincers of crabs on its temples. And this
> one too came from Rhodes.

Amphitrite was a sea goddess, the wife of Poseidon and queen of the oceans.
Since she was less known as a mythological figure, her statue was often
identified with Aphrodite, of whom the iconographical details do not fit. An
example of this confusion can be found in the *Parastaseis*, as quoted above, and
also in the following:[89]

> In the same Forum also stood an awe-inspiring statue of an elephant, in the
> area on the left near the great statue. This manifested a strange spectacle. For
> once there was an earthquake and the elephant fell over and broke one back
> foot. The soldiers of the prefect – for they used to guard the Forum – shouted
> to each other and came running to re-erect it, and found inside the same
> elephant all the bones of a complete human body, and a small box which had
> written on the top: 'Not even in death am I separated from the holy maiden

---

[86] *Parastaseis*, c. 38.   [87] Georgios Kedrenos, 344.2; after Constantine of Rhodes, v. 90–162.
[88] Themistios, *Oration*, 13, 176d.   [89] *Parastaseis*, c. 17.

Aphrodite.' The prefect added this to the public treasury for coins, in addition
to the above cases.

This statue is unknown from other sources. The forum stood on the site of an
ancient necropolis, so it may well have happened that old graves were sometimes hit during construction work, and that sarcophagi or caskets with bones in
them were found. But of course these were not inside a hollow-cast statue of an
elephant, and the inscription quoted here cannot have mentioned Aphrodite as
a maiden – but since it forms a correct hexameter, if her name is omitted and the
sequence of the last words changed, we may assume that her name was added by
the author of this anecdote, who thought that the statue in question actually
depicted her.

The third 'spectacle' of the *Parastaseis* deals with some statues and other
objects at the forum that were allegedly stolen by thieves in the time of
Constantine the Great, and reports that the thieves were executed. More interesting is the last part of this chapter:[90]

> There too after this Areios met his disgusting death, the wretch who dared to
> blaspheme worse than the pagans, the miserable creature who wanted to seize
> the patriarchal throne of Constantinople by imperial aid with procession and
> honour. But Alexander, great in divine knowledge, did not cease until he
> brought the man to his horrible death. So in that place about twenty-nine
> palms distant from the arch, Areios was represented in the reign of god-loving
> Theodosios, on a slab of marble close to the ground, and with him Sabellius,
> Makedonios and Eunomios, an object of disgust to passers-by, to vent on them
> dung and urine and spittle, and to load with dishonour those who had dishon-
> oured the Son of God. These things can be seen up to the present day by those
> who wish to examine what we have written with philosophy and effort.

Areios, a priest from Alexandria after whom the heresy of Arianism is named,
died suddenly in Constantinople on a procession in 335 when he passed the
Forum of Constantine.[91] But there is no reason to believe that this individual
was really depicted as a marble relief near the ground; we should rather assume
that a tomb slab from the old necropolis, which had been reused for paving the
forum, was interpreted in this way.

While the statue of Constantine fell from its column in 1106, the other statues
of the forum survived until the Fourth Crusade in 1204. In 1167 we hear of two
female statues of bronze over the western arch of the forum, which cannot be
identified from older sources: one of them was called by the people the
Hungarian, the other the Roman woman. When 'the Roman' fell from its pedes-
tal, Emperor Manuel I Komnenos gave an order to raise it up again and to pull

---

[90] *Parastaseis*, c. 39.   [91] Williams, *Arius*, pp. 80–1.

down 'the Hungarian', hoping to raise up the fortunes of the Romans in their war against the Hungarians.[92]

The statue of Athena in front of the Senate stood until 1203 when it was destroyed by a superstitious crowd shortly before the Crusaders' attack. Niketas Choniates describes it with these words:[93]

> The wine-bibbing portion of the vulgar masses smashed the statue of Athena that stood on a pedestal in the Forum of Constantine, for it appeared to the foolish rabble that she was beckoning on the Western armies. She rose to a standing height of thirty feet and wore a garment made of bronze, as was the entire figure. The robe reached down to her feet and fell into folds in many places so that no part of the body which Nature has ordained to be clothed should be exposed. A military girdle tightly cinctured her waist. Covering her prominent breasts and shoulders was an upper garment of goatskin embellished with the Gorgon's head. Her long bare neck was an irresistible delight to behold. The bronze was so transformed by its convincing portrayal of the goddess in all her parts that her lips gave the appearance that, should one stop to listen, one would hear a gentle voice. The veins were represented dilated as though fluid were flowing through their twisted ways to wherever needed throughout the whole body, which, though lifeless, appeared to partake of the full bloom of life. And the eyes were filled with deep yearning. On her head was set a helmet with horsehair crest, and terribly did it nod from above. Her braided hair tied in the back was a feast for the eyes, while the locks, falling loosely over the forehead, set off the braided tresses. Her left hand tucked up the folds of her dress while she pointed her right hand toward the south; her head was also gently turned southward, and her eyes also gazed in the same direction.

Athena usually had a spear in her right hand and a shield in her left, but is sometimes depicted without these attributes; for example in the statue called the Minerva from Arezzo, which looks very similar to what Niketas describes.[94]

When reporting the destruction of most ancient statues in Constantinople by the Crusaders in 1204, Niketas also mentions another statue on the forum:

> The Hera of bronze standing in the Forum of Constantine was cast into a smelting furnace and minted into coins; her head could barely be carted off to the Great Palace by four yokes of oxen.

Given its apparently monumental size, it is surprising that no other source refers to this piece.

---

[92] Niketas Choniates, p. 151.65–74.

[93] Ibid., pp. 558.41–559.73; the event is also mentioned by Robert de Clari, p. 110.

[94] Papamastorakis, 'Interpreting', p. 219. For an alternative explanation see Mathiopulu, 'Klassisches und Klassizistisches', pp. 32–6.

7 The Servant of the Wind

Halfway on the way west from the Forum of Constantine to that of Theodosios, a monumental tetrapylon with a high pyramidal roof stood at a place called the Bread Market (*Artopoleion*). Older sources call it the 'Tetrapylon of bronze', apparently on account of its sheeting by bronze plates with reliefs, while in later times the weathervane on its top – a winged statue of bronze on a globe that was held in balance by a waving mantle – gave the name 'servant of the wind' (*Anemodoulion*) to the whole building.[95] This is how the *Parastaseis* describe it:[96]

> Spectacle number four, which is in the buildings of the Bread Market. – A small dog, made out of marble, bearing many teats, as many as twenty, or lumps which they sought to worship, was visible for all who wanted to see from every side. And heads of a peacock and an eagle and a lioness and rams, and sparrows and crows and one turtle dove and a weasel and five heifers lowing and two Gorgons, one on the right and one on the left, one looking into the face of the other, carved from marble in relief and all mixed up together below the same buildings or Bread Market, as a spectacle, the work of Constantine. There was also an oxherd above an ox ploughing, as if intending to dig the earth, a great spectacle for those who saw it.

Except for the first object, the small marble she-dog, this text obviously refers to the reliefs on the bronze plates. The rest of the chapter claims that 'all these stories' were destroyed in the time of Emperor Zenon (474–91). It tells about a doctor and philosopher Galenos, who understands that the inscriptions near the two Gorgon heads predict Zenon's overthrow in 474, his denunciation after his return in 475 and execution. In reality, however, the reliefs survived; they are described by Constantine of Rhodes and Kedrenos, whose excerpt is, in this case, much shorter than the original text, and, at the occasion of its destruction by the Crusaders in 1204, by Niketas Choniates. Constantine says:[97]

> Let fifth place among the incomparable wonders be taken in my representation in words by the loftily soaring bronze construction, perhaps displaying the form of a tower-composed pyramid or the well-turned crest of a Persian tiara, which great Theodosios set up. It is an exceptional example of the sculptor's art, a four-legged structure full of wonder, fitted with four brazen sides, adorned on all sides both with carved creatures and tendrils bursting with fruits and small pomegranates. Naked Erotes tangled in vines stand there smiling sweetly and laughing from on high at those below; in contrast, other youths, kneeling, blow out the winds through bronze trumpets, one the west wind, and again another

---

[95] Anderson, 'Classified Knowledge'; Berger, *Untersuchungen*, pp. 312–6. The globe is mentioned by Robert de Clari, p. 108.
[96] *Parastaseis*, c. 40.   [97] Constantine of Rhodes, v. 178–201.

the south. At the summit of this, a monstruous creature made of bronze with bronze wings been blown around depict the sharp blasts of the winds and the gales that blow towards the city, the north wind, the south wind, and the fair northerly, the bold east wind, and the hard-blowing southerly.

Niketas Choniates describes the Anemodoulion in still greater detail, mentioning also scenes of agricultural life and fishery. Such a decoration is entirely out of place on a monument of this kind, and requires an explanation. A possible hint is given by the strange account in the *Patria* about the Anemodoulion:

> The bronze Anemodourin was set up by the impious Heliodoros in the time of Leon of Syrian origin, just as the twelve winds are set up there. The four large bronze works were brought from Dyrrhachion. A woman had them as her dowry from some temple. He made this with much knowledge of astronomy.

Heliodoros appears in the Life of Saint Leon of Catania, which is staged in the time of Leon III (717–41), as a sorcerer and adversary of the hero, and since Leon, being the first iconoclast emperor, enjoyed a bad reputation in later times, the attribution to him is rather surprising. But Benjamin Anderson noted that the name Anemodoulion and all references to the weathervane and the relief decoration appear only in texts after that date, and therefore suggested that a tetrapylon from the early Byzantine age may have been embellished by adding these parts, probably spolia, as a monument of victory after the failed siege of Constantinople by the Arabs in 717–18.[98] While some details of the decoration, such as the representation of the winds, would fit well into the few things we know about the art of this era, the Erotes or puttos entangled in vines and the pastoral scenes are still difficult to explain; it should also be noted that the building is called 'of bronze' from an earlier time.

8 The Rider on the Tauros

The Tauros or Forum of Theodosios I had, in addition to the triumphal column with the emperor's statue, two equestrian statues of his sons Arkadios and Honorios on ground level.[99] When the statue from the column had fallen down and Arkadios had been removed to serve as that of Justinian, only the statue of Honorios remained, but was soon not recognised as such. The *Parastaseis*, for example, write in their Chapter 66:

> You should know that the statue called Tauros is Theodosios the Great. It is here that the emperor once used to receive the leaders of barbarian peoples. It was formerly silver, as Sozomenos tells us. Clement says that the silver and manifold marble statues are of Constantine <and> his son Constans.

---

[98] Anderson, 'Leo III'.   [99] Effenberger, 'Reiterstandbilder'.

As at many other places in the *Parastaseis*, we learn that the statue was being identified with the name of the place where it stood, so that Theodosios was being called Tauros, whoever this person was. But since the statue of Theodosios (and Arkadios) had long since disappeared by the time the *Parastaseis* were written, the statue of Honorios must be meant here. Only the *Patria* speak in the present tense, in an addition to the text from the *Parastaseis*, about a statue of Theodosios on the column, and then go on:[100]

> His sons are above the lofty great quadruple columns: Honorios stands on the stone arch to the West, Arkadios on the stone arch to the East. In the middle of the courtyard is a huge equestrian statue, which some people call Joshua son of Nun, others Bellerophon. It was brought from Antioch the Great.

It is highly improbable that there were also statues of Arkadios and Honorios on the 'lofty great quadruple columns', that is, the two arches which gave access to the square – of which one has been excavated.[101] The equestrian statue is, again, that of Honorios. It must have been very similar to the one later known as Justinian at the Augoustaion, and therefore clearly recognisable as that of a Roman emperor, not as a person from the Old Testament or from ancient Greek mythology.

Constantine of Rhodes identifies the equestrian statue as Theodosios I, mentions his wars against the usurper Maximos and the Skythians in Thrace, and describes horse and rider vividly and in great detail. In the report about its destruction by the Crusaders in 1204, which appears both at the appropriate place of his *History* and in the section *On the Statues* at its end, Niketas Choniates paraphrases the entry of the *Patria*, and explains the identifications proposed there:[102]

> Some maintained that it was of Joshua, son of Nun, conjecturing that his hand was pointed towards the sun as it sank in the west, commanding it to stand still upon Gabaon. The majority were of the opinion that it was Bellerophontes, born and bred in the Peloponnesos, mounted on Pegasos; the horse was unbridled, as was Pegasos, who, according to tradition, ran freely over the plains, spurning every rider, for he could both fly through the air and race over the land.

Of course, there is no reason to believe that this statue actually came from Antioch in Syria, as the *Patria* claim. After a remark on the inscriptions on the plinth of the rider, which predict the conquest of the city by the Russians (Rhos), the text says:

> And that impediment, which is the very short man-shaped bronze object tied in a kneeling position under the left foot of the huge horse, signifies the same as that which is depicted there.

---

[100] *Patria*, 2.47.   [101] Naumann, 'Neue Beobachtungen'.
[102] The version quoted here is that of *On the Statues*.

Figure 8 The column and statues on the Tauros forum.

Credit: Drawing by Ulrich Reuter, Berlin, in Effenberger, 'Reiterstandbilder', p. 287.

The 'impediment' can easily be identified as a small figure of a barbarian under the horse's hoof. Such figures were often placed under the raised foot of a horse to support it, as can be seen on coins from the Roman age that depict equestrian statues – but this one is interpreted as a device of sympathetic magic to keep possible invaders under control. In *On the Statues* the passage has been expanded as follows:

> There was an ancient tradition which came down to us and which was in the mouths of all, that under this horse's front left hoof there was buried the image of a man which, as it had been handed down to some, was of a certain Venetian; others claimed that it was of a member of some other Western nation not allied with the Romans, or that it was of a Bulgarian. As the attempt

was often made to secure the hoof, the statue beneath was completely covered over and hidden from sight. When the horse was broken into pieces and committed to the flames, together with the rider, the statue was found buried beneath the horse's hoof; it was dressed in the kind of cloak that is woven from sheep's wool. Showing little concern over what was said about it, the Latins cast it also into the fire.

Finally, let us also have a look on another 'statue' on the Tauros that is mentioned elsewhere in the *Patria*:[103]

> But also an enchanted couch with mosquito curtains (*konopion*) stood on top of the western arch of the Tauros. The mosquito, the fly and the bug were made from bronze, and because of them these insects did not affect the city. Emperor Basileios crushed them.

Since the only source that mentions this object, also claims that it was already destroyed, there is every reason to believe that it never existed.

9 The Place of Brotherly Love

Some 500 metres west of the Tauros, at a gate to the northwest and where a major street to the Church of the Apostles branched off from the main avenue to the Golden Gate, lay the Capitol of Constantinople. Given its obviously pagan character, it must go back to the first phase of Constantinople when Constantine the Great tried to establish a syncretistic cult of pagan and Christian elements.

The Capitol is first mentioned in 407, then in 425, when it was turned into a law school, and only rarely thereafter. Later sources mostly call it 'the place of brotherly love', obviously referring to the two pairs of porphyry statues of emperors (carried off to Venice after 1204 and now standing at the Church of San Marco in Venice) embracing each other in its eastern portico.[104] This is what the *Parastaseis* say about them:[105]

> The so-called Philadelphion is the sons of Constantine the Great. One of them arrived in Constantinople from Gaul after his father's death. They greeted each other with a great meeting and rejoicing, and at once they erected statues of themselves in the city preserving this scene.

In reality, Constantine the Great had only three surviving sons, not four, and they fought against each other until only Konstantios II was left as the only Roman emperor. Clearly, the embracing statues do not depict them, but rather the first four Tetrarchs, Diocletian, Maximianus, Galerius and Constans.

---

[103] *Patria*, 3.200.
[104] Laubscher, 'Beobachtungen'; Bassett, *Urban Image*, p. 242; Niewöhner and Peschlow, 'Tetrarchenfiguren'; Effenberger, 'Wiederverwendung'.
[105] *Parastaseis*, c. 70.

The two groups of embracing emperors were carved from one piece of porphyry each, together with the monumental columns where they had stood halfway up on small consoles. The figures are slightly under life size and wear the military costume of their time, with armour, cloak and Pannonian cap. A fragment from the missing foot on one Tetrarch, which has been replaced at San Marco, has been found in Istanbul.[106]

For a long time it was assumed that the columns stood in the eastern porch of the Capitol until 1204.[107] New investigations have shown, however, that the Tetrarchs must have already been separated from their columns when these were brought to Constantinople:[108] one of the columns was cut horizontally above and below the figures, the other with oblique vertical cuts so that an obelisk or pillar could be carved out of it. This latter must be the four-sided porphyry pillar at the Capitol which lost its cross during a thunderstorm in 407, and since free-standing monuments with crosses are not attested before the age of Theodosios I (379–95), the Tetrarchs must have been brought during Theodosios' time from Thessalonica, where he resided before coming to Constantinople in 380.

On this occasion, the figures were adapted to the imperial iconography of their age: diadems and imperial brooches of metal were attached to the figures, as can be seen from the fixing holes, and beards were picked into the faces of one emperor of each pair. Also, one pair has been cut in two pieces, the other not. This suggests that the figures were now shown as Theodosios I with the western emperors Gratian and Valentinian II, and that the fourth – the most damaged figure – was kept separately, and reunited with the others only in Venice. The identification with the sons of Constantine, then, belongs to a still later age.

The noses and ears of all four figures are intentionally mutilated – we do not know when and for what reason, but in any case this shows they were not always interpreted as Christian emperors – even in Constantinople.

In the late Byzantine age, the Tetrarchs had long since disappeared and in their place two emperors sitting on thrones are mentioned by the sources. A Russian pilgrim calls them the 'righteous judges',[109] and Manuel Chrysoloras speaks in 1411 about,[110]

> the statues of porphyry which sit on thrones at the meeting of three streets, and therefore have been given the designation as market inspectors and supervisors.

[106] Naumann, 'Rundbau', pp. 209–11.
[107] For example, in Berger, *Untersuchungen*, pp. 330–7, 347.
[108] Niewöhner and Peschlow, 'Tetrarchenfiguren'; Effenberger, 'Wiederverwendung'.
[109] Majeska, *Russian Travelers*, p. 145.   [110] Manuel Chrysoloras, c. 49.

Figure 9 The Tetrarchs of San Marco.
Credit: Photograph courtesy of Franz Alto Bauer.

10 Empress Helena and the Lord of Amastris

Perhaps the most mysterious site of Byzantine Constantinople is *ta Amastrianou*, that is, the house or place 'of the man from Amastris'. This was apparently a rectangular square, surrounded by colonnades, on the southern side of the main street, the Mese, roughly opposite to the Capitol on its northern side. A semicircular courtyard in the south connected it to a monumental rotunda, probably the entrance hall of a palace which can be dated to the first decades of the fifth century (this palace can perhaps be identified with that of Arkadia listed by the *Notitia urbis Constantinopolitae* in its ninth region).[111] The rotunda collapsed at an unknown time, and its trunk was later turned into a cistern with a platform on top on which a small new palace was built. This palace was converted into the Myrelaion monastery by Emperor Romanos I Lakapenos (920–44), with a church added on a separate substructure.[112] The trunk of the rotunda and the church do still exist, while nothing has remained of the square in front of it, and of its decoration with statues.

These statues are described by a number of sources. I will begin here with Chapter 41 of the *Parastaseis*, which is apparently compiled from several sources and therefore mentions some statues more than once:[113]

> Spectacle number five, that of *ta Amastrianou*, by Caracallus the praepositus. – The spectacle or statue, the idol of the city of Byzantium, dating from the reign of Trajan, as Mekas and Glaukos relate, on whose writings Theodore the chronographer depends. In this place was Zeus Helios on a chariot inlaid with marble, the staffbearer of Zeus, Aristides, the reclining Herakles, a charioteer of the gods with the inscription 'Apollo Pankrates'. There was the river Kytlos, the eagle worshipped by a wolf; there are tortoises full of birds and among them eighteen she-serpents.

The second part of the chapter is very corrupted and difficult to understand, and talks about a statue only here:

> In this place attacks and falls of demons happened, like to emperors, to the philosophers, especially if the accursed emperors were fornicators in word or offspring. For this reason let them pay attention to the naked statue; and you should cook the iron herb with a small spoon and roast it with the nostrils, and suckle it at the friends of the emperor.

It seems that also Chapter 44 of the *Parastaseis* refers to *ta Amastrianou*:[114]

> Near the so-called Steelyard (*stater*), which is called *molion*, was a fox made of Peganousian marble, its length five cubits and its width two and a half cubits. In a southerly direction lay an imperial house, and in a northerly direction the old temple. On its chest inlaid in gold and silver letters was written 'Aphrodite Selene'. It was given to the Persians by way of tribute at the time of the Emperor Anastasius, in place of a thousand pounds of silver.

Molion is apparently a wrong reading of *modion*, that is, a bushel. It refers to an antique relief of an altar with a fire burning on it, which was misinterpreted as a bushel with grain spikes, and had at both sides field signs showing hands on spears. It decorated the entrance to *ta Amastrianou* from the main street in the north, and is described in *Parastaseis* Chapter 12. The old temple in the north,

---

[111] Niewöhner and Abura, 'Rundbau', pp. 435–7.   [112] Striker, *Myrelaion*.
[113] *Parastaseis*, c. 41.   [114] *Parastaseis*, c. 44.

then, must be the Capitol, and the 'imperial house' to the south is the palace to which the big rotunda belonged.[115] The marble of this statue came from the small island Peganousia, near Prokonnesos in the Sea of Marmara, and is mentioned very rarely. The *orgyia* must here be a cubit, not a fathom as some have suggested, so that the statue was more than 2 metres, but not 9 metres long.[116]

The question is, as in many other cases in the *Parastaseis*, where did the author of the chapter find this information about a statue that had disappeared more than two hundred years earlier? Again, we have the choice to believe that he either had a now lost source at his disposal, or that he invented the story – not the part about the statue itself, but about the way it was lost.

Chapter 41 of the *Parastaseis* is quoted in the *Patria*, where its first part is shortened drastically:[117]

> In the place of the Amastrianon stood Zeus Helios on a chariot of marble, and a reclining Herakles. There was also a river worshipped by a wolf, and tortoises full of birds and eighteen sheserpents.

The second part is omitted completely and replaced by this text:

> And the standing marble statue of a lord who came from the land of Paphlagonia, and another one, buried in dung and urine and dust, the slave of the Paphlagonian from Amastris. Both were sacrificed to the demons at this place and set up as a source of wonder. There is also an adornment of slender columns, erected in a hemicycle. Many apparitions of demons occurred there.

The 'slender columns in a hemicycle' must be the curved forecourt of the rotunda (a small part of its back wall still exists under a modern hotel building).

Another description of *ta Amastrianou* is that in the chronicle of Georgios Kedrenos, again based on a lost poem by Constantine of Rhodes:[118]

> *Ta Amastrianou* is called either after a humble man who had Amastris as his home town and came to the city because of his poverty and died there, or because of the actively working bad reputation of the place, for every evildoer and murderer gets his punishment there, and has received this most shameful name because of the disgusting behaviour of the Paphlagonians.
> Once there was a very big temple of Helios and Selene to whose northern side columns stood in a row with a recess in the middle like a well-rounded niche. On top of them there was Helios on a white chariot, while Selene, crowned like a bride, was sitting on a coach. These were the works of Byzas, the husband of Pheidaleia. Below, near the foundations of the building, sat a scepter-bearer on a throne, commanding the people to obey their rulers.

---

[115] Berger, 'Haus'.

[116] For the relation between cubit and fathom, see Schreiner, 'Untersuchungen'.

[117] *Patria*, 2.29.   [118] Georgios Kedrenos, c. 344.13.

> Near the ground was a figure of Zeus from white stone, a work of Pheidias, which seemed to sit on a couch.

It is not easy to understand from these texts how many statues stood at *ta Amastrianou*, who they represented, and what all this has to do with the town of Amastris in Paphlagonia. Most but not all statues mentioned in Chapter 41 of the *Parastaseis* can be identified with those in the other sources.

The fact that Constantine of Rhodes makes two alternative proposals to explain the name *ta Amastrianou*, both without connection to the statues at this place or to the architecture, suggests that he had no idea about its real origin. The mention of a standing marble statue of a 'lord from Paphlagonia' in the *Patria*, however, leads us to the right solution, for it suggests that an ancient statue, probably the most important one of the whole ensemble, actually showed a Paphlagonian, that is, a man from Amastris. This statue may well be the 'idol of the city of Byzantium' of the *Parastaseis*, where it figures prominently at the beginning of Chapter 41. Its description as *theamation* or *eidoleion* does probably not mean, as assumed by Cameron and Herrin,[119] that it was small in size.

It has been observed long ago that two *ta Amastrianou* statues are depicted on coins from Amastris in the Roman age,[120] and some more have recently been added to this list.[121] One of these statues is Apollo, who is shown on the coins as a naked standing figure with an arch in one hand and an unguent flask (*aryballos*) in the other.[122] This is, without doubt, the 'idol of Byzantium', the 'lord from Paphlagonia' or the 'man from Amastris', and should also be identified with the naked statue in the second part of *Parastaseis* Chapter 41.

The 'charioteer of the gods with the inscription Apollo *Pankrates*' in the same chapter makes no sense; probably the phrase combines two marginal glosses which have crept into the text, of which the first referred to the statue of Zeus Helios, the second to the naked Apollo. The original epithet may have been *Pankratiastes*, thus referring to the ancient Greek *pankration* – a combat sport similar to what we call today mixed martial arts – but is never actually attested in this form.[123]

Only in the entry of the *Patria*, the 'lord from Paphlagonia' has a slave who lies in the garbage on the ground. The courtyard of *ta Amastrianou* was used for centuries as a market and place of execution, so it is well possible that its pavement was covered by a thick layer of waste and debris, as is attested for the Strategion in the eleventh century,[124] and that a statue in a low position was

[119] Cameron and Herrin, *Constantinople*, p. 111.   [120] Von Schlosser, 'Münzbilder', pp. 22–8.
[121] Von Mosch, 'Sandalenlöser'.   [122] Ibid., pp. 119–25.
[123] Von Mosch, 'Sandalenlöser', p. 121.   [124] Ioannes Skylitzes, p. 482.84–7.

Figure 10 Coin of Marcus Aurelius from Amastris, showing Apollo on the reverse side. https://gallica.bnf.fr/ark:/12148/btv1b8561152b.

Credit: Bibliothèque nationale de France.

half-buried in it. Since the supposed slave is described as lying, he may have been, in the worst case, the reclining Herakles, who will be discussed below.

A statue of Zeus Helios on a chariot of marble is mentioned by all these texts, and since Helios is also shown on coins from Amastris, it may also have come from there.[125] Only Constantine of Rhodes claims that at *ta Amastrianou* was the goddess Selene also crowned like a bride and sitting on a coach,[126] so some doubt may be allowed whether it actually existed – but it must be admitted that such a representation would fit perfectly well to the hypothesis that a cult of Constantine's mother Helena was established there (see below).

The next statues mentioned in *Parastaseis* Chapter 41 are the 'staffbearer of Zeus' and Aristides. Possibly this refers to only one object, and Aristides *is* the staffbearer. He is clearly an invented person, who also appears in the preceding chapter as a philosopher, and elsewhere in the text as architect of the Kynegion, a place of pagan magical practices.[127] The staffbearer is probably not Hermes in his classical iconography, as has been assumed,[128] but the sceptre-bearing man on a throne mentioned by Georgios Kedrenos.

---

[125] Von Mosch, 'Sandalenlöser', p. 121.
[126] The phrase ἡ δ᾽ αὖ Σελήνη νυμφικῶς ἐστεμμένη (reading δ᾽ for the δὲ in Kedrenos) is a perfect Byzantine dodecasyllabus.
[127] See Section 1 above.
[128] *Parastaseis*, comment at Cameron and Herrin, *Constantinople*, p. 225.

The following mention in the *Parastaseis* to the reclining Herakles and the river god refers most probably the same object which should be identified with the personification of the Meles river which can be seen on ancient coins from Amastris.[129] This must also be the reclining Zeus in Kedrenos. No text after his chronicle mentions *ta Amastrianou* by name, but it seems that a reclining Herakles has survived into the late Byzantine age, for in 1411 Manuel Chrysoloras mentions a statue 'from white stone or marble, a bit above the bank of the river flowing through the city, which seems to rest on its elbow'.[130] The river is the Lykos which flowed through the west of Constantinople and ended in the Theodosian harbour, about 300 metres west of *ta Amastrianou*.

The next statue in the list in *Parastaseis* Chapter 41 is the 'river Kytlos', which should probably be identified with the Lykos. Personifications of rivers or river gods are usually shown as figures reclining with one arm on a big jar from which water flows out, so it is tempting to identify this object as also the reclining Herakles mentioned before.

Hans-Christoph von Mosch has drawn our attention to another group of statues that may have ended up at *ta Amastrianou*.[131] Dionysios of Halikarnassos describes a group of statues from the forum of Lavinium, an old city near Rome, which was, according to tradition, founded by Aeneas himself.[132] The group commemorated Lavinium's foundation and consisted of an eagle, a she-wolf and a fox fighting for the fire of Vesta. Von Mosch believes that this group also included the fox in *Parastaseis* Chapter 44, and that its inscription 'Aphrodite Selene' shows its dedication to the old Phoenician moon goddess, which was an important part of the ancestry myths of empresses who wanted to be seen as members of the *gens Iulia*. The group's function in Constantinople, therefore, must have been to align Constantine's mother, Helena, with Aphrodite Selene to make her humble origins socially acceptable. This argument is convincing except for one objection: Dionysios speaks of bronze statues, whereas at least the fox at *ta Amastrianou* was made of marble. We should assume therefore, as in other cases, that the originals had stayed at their place and Constantinople was decorated with copies.

Little can be said about the other statues mentioned by the *Parastaseis*. We do not know what the 'tortoises full of birds and eighteen she-serpents' looked like and what their meaning was. A philosopher called Koukountios is entirely

---

[129] Von Schlosser, 'Münzbilder', p. 25.   [130] Manuel Chrysoloras, c. 49.
[131] Von Mosch, 'Aphrodite Selene'.   [132] Antiquitates romanae, 1.59.

unknown,[133] and it is unclear whether he was depicted alone or with the members of his family, whom he allegedly sacrificed to the pagan gods. If his statue or a group of statues existed at all, it certainly represented somebody completely different.

But what was the reason why such an ensemble of statues was set up at this place? If von Mosch is right, only Constantine the Great himself can have brought these statues to Constantinople, thus connecting the cult of Zeus Helios to himself and that of Aphrodite Selene to his mother Helena, and adding the statues of Lavinium as representants of one of the antecessor cities of Rome. The statues of *ta Amastrianou* then corresponded to the statues of the Capitol which lay nearby, just across the main avenue.

But this creates another problem: *ta Amastrianou* lay in front of a palace from the early fifth century, while its semi-pagan decoration only makes sense if dated one century earlier. Von Mosch believed that the statues of *ta Amastrianou* originally stood in the Capitol. In fact, if the courtyard of *ta Amastrianou* was built under Constantine, together with the Capitol and as a pendant to it, and had nothing to do with the palace – which was a separate building and only connected to it by the semicircular portico mentioned in the *Patria* – then it seems more logical that the statues were placed in *ta Amastrianou* from the time they arrived in Constantinople. In other words, the name *ta Amastrianou* is derived from the statue of Apollo *Pankratiastes*, the 'man from Amastris', and refers only to the courtyard originally dedicated to the Empress Helena as Aphrodite Selene, not to the fifth-century palace or to the house built on its trunk after the rotunda had collapsed.

11 The Ox of Bronze

Although a number is missing, the sixth spectacle of the list must be the one given in Chapter 42 of the *Parastaseis*:

> About the Ox. – We will describe clearly to you the spectacle at the Ox, which you have frequently asked us in letters to make clear to you, Philokalos. We know that it was built in the Hippodrome by Valentinian the Praepositus of Constans.

Here we have another case in which the *Parastaseis* claim that a statue was moved from one place in Constantinople to another. The text then goes on:

> And there is an enormous great furnace, preserved until the present day, where Julian, hated of God, burned many Christians on the pretext of their

---

[133] Misread as Koukobytios by the editor T. Preger; the name may be a corruption of Iucundus or Secundus.

being criminals. The furnace bore as a spectacle a huge bronze ox, in imitation of which that at the Neorion harbour was made.

We know from the fifth-century *Notitia urbis Constantinopolitanae* that actually an ox or bull of bronze stood in this region, probably as decoration of a cattle market. Statues of animals are occasionally mentioned in Constantinople and sometimes gave their names to churches, such as Saint Julian of the Partridge and Saint Prokopios of the Tortoise, or to the home for aged people called the Rams.[134] The tortoise referred to by Ioannes Malalas and Hesychios of Miletus in the sixth century, as well as a group of storks, and ascribed to Apollonios of Tyana, has been mentioned earlier.[135]

In the case of the ox of bronze on the marketplace in Constantinople, the *Parastaseis* claim that it was not a mere decoration but used for executions. It is connected to the legend of Phalaris, tyrant of Agrigentum in Sicily in the sixth century BC, who murdered his guests in such a bull-shaped furnace.[136] The concept of a glowing bronze ox as a device for executions finally entered the Christian tradition, and death in such an ox is later ascribed to a whole row of martyrs, beginning with Antipas of Pergamon – a person mentioned in the Apocalypse of John.

By suggesting that the furnace was not shaped like an ox but only decorated with a statue, the author of the *Parastaseis* partially misunderstood the tradition, and the *Patria* make it worse by speaking of a furnace with the head of an ox on it. But let us go on with the quote from the *Parastaseis*:

> An air of disgrace attached to the bronze ox because of the burning, up to the reign of the wicked Phokas. But after Phokas himself was burnt the Ox was melted down by Herakleios for the treasury of the guards and went to Pontus for army recruitment, since the guardpost was in Pontus. It was worth twenty-four measures of silver, because it was cast. And this remains here even up to the present day for people to see, cast into frowning imperial portraits.

We know that Emperor Phokas (602–10), as well as some other persons after him, were executed at this place – but the Greek expression ἐν τῷ Βοΐ can mean not only 'on the square of the Ox' but also 'in the Ox', and so suggested that the ox of bronze, which may have actually been melted down under Herakleios (610–41) to make coins of it,[137] was used to torture Phokas to death.

Over the centuries, the story of the ox of bronze was more and more attached to the Christian saints, and the final result is this short entry in Georgios Kedrenos:[138]

---

[134] *Parastaseis*, c. 26; *Patria*, 2.23, 3.62, 3.69.   [135] See Section 1 above.
[136] Bianchetti, *Falaride*, pp. 55–68.   [137] Speck, 'Bronze'.   [138] Georgios Kedrenos, 344.12.

The bull of bronze came from Pergamon, and it was a furnace in which the holy martyr Antipas was burned.

12 Three-Headed Statues

At this point, we should expect in the *Parastaseis* a last spectacle on the list of seven. But not only is the number missing, as in the previous entry, the text also jumps to another place in the city:[139]

> See the wonder of the Milion by the official Dioscorus, from the things to be seen in the reign of the Emperor Maurice.

This title does not fit to the following text where neither the Milion nor the Emperor Maurice are mentioned, and was probably misunderstood earlier in a preceding manuscript.[140] The following story is completely garbled, but instructive:

> The explanation of the name of the so-called Senate of the Forum is none other than that Senatos built the Senate. And the porphyry statue there of three stones with three heads, which some said was of Constantine the Great in the middle, Constantius on the left and Constans on the right, with two feet, but six hands – a strange spectacle for those who saw it, each one looking in a different direction – and one head.

Deities with three heads were represented in ancient Greek art either by a three-faced head on a single body, or by figures with three complete upper bodies and six arms.[141] Hecate, the goddess of the Underworld, was often depicted in this way, and she was greatly revered in ancient Byzantium, since she had saved, according to tradition, the city from a siege by Alexander the Great's father, Philip II of Macedon, in 340/39 BC.[142] But male deities were sometimes also shown with three heads or upper bodies, as were monsters of hell, such as Kerberos and Skylla. The object described here was certainly a male god with three upper bodies, while a three-headed monster is mentioned at the Exakionion, and will be discussed in the following section.

The text of *Parastaseis* Chapter 43 then goes on:

> But once there was a fire in this place, and while everyone was busy (so to speak) that extraordinary thing was stolen, in the reign of Theodosios the Younger, the son of Arcadius, who immediately made threats through a herald in the suburbs and districts by the sea if the spectacle were not

---

[139] *Parastaseis*, c. 43.

[140] The manuscript has Ζήτει τοῦ Μιλίου τοῦ θεάματος τοῦ ὀφικίου Διοσκόρου· ἐκ τῶν καθόραν ἐπὶ Μαυρικίου αὐγούστου. Cameron and Herrin, *Constantinople*, p. 117 read, '<Spectacle number> seven. From the Milion a spectacle of the ? official Dioskoros.'

[141] Kirfel, *Dreiköpfige Gottheit*.   [142] Newskaja, *Byzanz*, p. 131; Russell, *Byzantium*, pp. 65–9.

found. Those who dared to do this were not able to remove it to their own country, but were overtaken by the emperor's boat and did away with themselves; they cast both the spectacle and themselves into the sea and were drowned. And although many boats and rope-baskets and some divers came because of the anguish of the emperor, and though he offered a multitude of gifts and with fearful oaths promised to give five hundred centenaria to anyone who could rescue it from the sea, no one succeeded in doing so. Then this Theodosios in anger gave over the house of Senatos to the fire which was supported by four columns.

Let us state here that the whole story is about a statue which no longer exists, and that in this story Theodosios II (408–50) gives an order to burn a building that had actually been destroyed by fire at an earlier date. The mention of four columns identifies the building with the Senate at the forum, which did not burn in his time and was later only damaged by the great fire of 465. Since Constantine of Rhodes had confused it, as mentioned before, with the other Senate building near the emperor's palace, we may assume the same here; this other Senate, the predecessor of the so-called Magnaura, burned down in 403, before Theodosios' reign began.

Another story about a three-headed statue stands in the so-called *Continuation of Theophanes*: when a 'godless and savage people' attacked the empire in the reign of Emperor Theophilos (829–42), his friend and counsellor Patriarch Ioannes Grammatikos (837–43) used magical practices to connect their three leaders with a three-headed bronze statue in the Hippodrome. Three men with big iron hammers were sent to the Hippodrome by night and tried to cut off the statue's heads. While two heads actually fell off, the third was only slightly deformed. As a result, a civil war broke out between the three leaders, in which two of them died, and only the third survived in bad health.[143] In this case, the story was obviously invented long after Ioannes' death with the intention of discrediting him – Ioannes was deposed soon after the emperor's death because of his religious policy, while the *Continuation of Theophanes* was written more than a hundred years later. The 'barbarian people' of the story is not called by name, and the attempt to identify them with the Russians is not convincing.[144]

13 Exakionion and Golden Gate

When the first land walls of Constantinople were built in the age of Constantine the Great, the main gate was established on the road leading to Thrace. Its name in later sources is the Exakionion, 'with six columns', probably because it had

---

[143] *Theophanes continuatus*, 4.7.   [144] See Mango, 'Antique statuary', note 41.

a facade with six columns in the upper storey.[145] Nothing is left of this gate today, and there is very little information about its statues. The most interesting among them is, in *Parastaseis* Chapter 21, another three-headed statue:

> The so-called Exakionion once held a hare, a hound and a huge Nimrod, all three of one piece of iron, and many other spectacles were preserved in this place.

This object belonged to a rare but still well-attested ancient iconographical type, that of a monster with three heads of a wolf, a lion and a dog that grew out of a dog's body, with a snake wound around it[146] – just that the wolf with laid-back ears was mistaken as a hare, and the lion as a bearded human face. Why the latter is identified as the biblical figure Nimrod is unknown. Major objects of art made of iron are occasionally attested, but were rare due to their complicated production.[147]

The second walls of Constantinople were constructed under Theodosios II (408–50) further to the west, between 408 and 413, and a monumental gate of white marble was added on the main street around 425, the so-called Golden Gate, which still exists as part of an Ottoman fortress.[148] A number of sources mention a group of elephants standing on top of it, beginning with the *Patria*:[149]

> The statues of the elephants of the Golden Gate were brought from the temple of Ares in Athens by Theodosios the Younger.

The chronicle of Georgios Kedrenos connects them to Theodosios I instead:[150]

> And the elephants which are on the Golden Gate are similar to those on which Theodosios once entered the city.

The elephants are last mentioned by Robert de Clari in 1204, who gives their number as two.[151] All speculation that they were once yoked to a chariot, or that this chariot was a quadriga and the elephants originally four, cannot be proved due to a lack of sources.

14 Prophecies of the Future

Let us now return to the city centre, and have a look on the Strategion, the 'general's place' or 'parade-ground' in the harbour area near the Golden Horn. This public square probably existed before the foundation of Constantinople,

---

[145] Berger, *Untersuchungen*, p. 352–6.   [146] Kirfel, *Dreiköpfige Gottheit*, pp. 128–31.
[147] One example from Constantinople is the statue of Emperor Anastasios I in the Hippodrome, on which see below Section 17.1.
[148] Asutay-Effenberger, *Landmauer*, pp. 54–61.   [149] *Patria*, 2.58.
[150] Georgios Kedrenos, c. 344.15. On Theodosios I and the elephants, see Section 4 above.
[151] Robert de Clari, p. 108.

but was developed and equipped with statues thereafter. While in Chapter 69 of the *Parastaseis* the name Strategion is used for an ancient tripod, it is applied to a statue in the *Patria*:[152]

> The statue called Strategion, which stands on the great square, is Alexander of Macedonia. It stood previously in Chrysopolis, as he had offered his army double pay for one year there. And because of this it was called Chrysopolis (golden city) by the Macedonians, and was called Strategion on account of the army. The statue stood in Chrysopolis, as the people had set it up, for 648 years, but Constantine the Great brought it into the city. Soldiers were dismissed there, for the place was flat.

Alexander the Great (339–323 BC) had, of course, never set foot in Byzantium, but is connected to the city by various legends. After some words about the fragment of an obelisk on the square, the text goes on:

> On the same Strategion also stood the tripod which has the past, the present and the future on it; the southern celestial sky and the basin of the tripod which was set up at *ta Steirou*, for the place was an oracle; and nearby the Tyche of the city. The Caesar Bardas, the uncle of Emperor Michael, removed, disassembled and destroyed them. The chronographer tells the history of the obelisk. The small Strategios is the statue of Leomakelles.

No other source mentions that Bardas, who acted as regent for his nephew Michael III from 856 to 866, removed these objects from the Strategion, and a statue of Leomakelles or 'Leon the Butcher', that is Leon I (457–74), called the 'small Strategios' is unknown. Of the other objects mentioned, only the 'southern celestial sky' may have been a statue, or rather a group of statues representing star signs of the southern sky such as the Centaur, the Altar and the river Eridnos, which would have been visualised as a river god.

15 Testing Chastity

In the popular perception, enchanted statues not only foretold the future, but sometimes also had other capabilities. The *Patria* contain two stories about statues that were used for tests of chastity. The first of them is connected to the big hospital of Emperor Theophilos (829–42), which, according to the tradition, replaced an old brothel from the time of Constantine the Great.[153] The story goes as follows:[154]

> On the hospital of Theophilos. – Constantine the Great built the big hospital building that can be seen on top of the hill, near the so-called

---

[152] *Parastaseis*, c. 69; *Patria*, 2.59.   [153] Berger, *Untersuchungen*, pp. 484–6.
[154] *Patria*, 3.65.

Zeugma, as a brothel. A statue of Aphrodite stood there on a braided stone column. Lovers went there and consorted with the adulterous women living there, for there was no other brothel than this house nor such adulterous women elsewhere. Inside the house were compartments separated at the columns with rings and curtains, and in this way the profligate lovers enjoyed themselves. The statue was a touchstone for chaste women and virgins, both rich and poor, who were held in suspicion. If someone defiled a girl's virginity, and many or few of them did not admit this, their parents and friends would say to them: 'Let's go to the statue of Aphrodite, and you will be tested as to whether you are chaste.' When they approached the place below the column, if she was without blame, she passed by unharmed, but if she was defiled or her virginity destroyed, a sudden apparition would confuse her, reluctantly and against her will, as soon as they approached the column with the statue, and lifting her dress in front of all, she would show her genitals to all. A similar phenomenon befell married women, if they had secretly committed adultery. And all were amazed, and all believed when the women confessed the adultery they had committed. The sister-in-law of the former *kouropalates* Justin smashed this statue, for her genitals too had been revealed when she had committed adultery and had passed by on horseback en route to the bath of the Blachernai, because an extraordinary rain had fallen, and it was impossible to go in the imperial galleys.

This is a wonderful anecdote, but probably without any real background. A sister of Emperor Justin II (565–78) is unknown to any other source. The second such story in the *Patria* is told about a portico called the Keratoembolin:[155]

Saint Andrew came to Byzantium before Constantine the Great, built a house at *ta Armatiou* and settled there. He made a cross with his own hands, cutting it from stone and doing the reliefs, and set it up in Saint Eirene the Old. Then he came to the Neorin to the portico called Keratoembolin, and taught.

The portico is given this name because a bronze arch was there, and on top of it stood a statue which had four horns on its head. And a miracle always happened there: if someone suspected that he was horned he would go there and approach the statue. If it was as he had assumed, the statue turned around three times. If it was not as he suspected, it stood quietly, and in this way the horned men were revealed.

Keratoembolin means 'portico with horns' or 'horned portico' and probably refers to a curved portico along the waterfront of the Neorin harbour on the Golden Horn. The story here plays with the popular Greek word *keratas*, which means 'horned' in the sense of 'cuckolded'.[156]

---

[155] *Patria*, 3.179.   [156] Berger, *Untersuchungen*, pp. 692–5.

16 Collections of Statues

16.1 Hagia Sophia

The *Parastaseis* report on a large collection of statues that once stood at the place where Hagia Sopha now rises:[157]

> At the Great Church which is now called Hagia Sophia, 427 statues were removed, most of them pagans. Among the many were those of Zeus, and of Carus, the ancestor of Diocletian, and the Zodiac, and Selene and Aphrodite and the star Arcturus, supported by two Persian statues, and the southern celestial sky and a priestess of Athene, soothsaying to the philosopher Hero, in profile. There were only a few of Christians, about eighty. Out of the many it is worth mentioning a few: Constantine, Constantius, Constans, Galen the quaestor, <caesar Julian and another Julian, a prefect> emperor Licinius, Valentinianus, Theodosios and Arcadius his son, Serapion the *consularis*, and three of Helena, the mother of Constantine: one of porphyry and of other marbles, one with silver inlay on a bronze column, one of ivory, given by Kypros the rhetor. These statues Justinian distributed about the city when he built the Great Church with faith and effort. Those who know the foregoing find a good number of them if they go round the city and look for them.

Like the legendary *Narrative of the Construction of Hagia Sophia*, the text implies that no building stood on the spot before Emperor Justinian, ignoring the two previous buildings from the fourth and early fifth century. If there is any truth in this account, the statues must have stood on the Augoustaion square south of it, as Sarah Bassett has pointed out.[158] A statue of Constantine's mother Helena on a short porphyry column is, in fact, mentioned on this square by early Byzantine sources, as for example by Ioannes Malalas:[159]

> He also built a basilica and great columns and statues in front of it, which he called Senate, and opposite to it he placed on a short porphyry column a statue of his mother Helena as Augusta, and called the square Augoustaion.

The number of statues, however, must be highly exaggerated, and we should ask ourselves which of them stood in the original source, and which were added by later legend. The remark at the end, that many statues of the city had once been there, is simply an attempt to make the account more plausible as is the reference to two groups of statues that actually stood elsewhere, the southern celestial sky on the Strategion, as mentioned, and the Zodiac in the Hippodrome.[160]

---

[157] *Parastaseis*, c. 11. The words in angle brackets are added from the quote in *Patria* 2.96.
[158] Bassett, *Urban Image*, pp. 74, 146–8.
[159] Ioannes Malalas, 13.7; also in *Chronicon paschale* p. 529.2–3; Hesychios, c. 39.
[160] See Section 17.4 below.

16.2 The baths of Zeuxippos

Perhaps the most famous collection of ancient statues in Constantinople was housed in the baths of Zeuxippos in the very heart of the city, next to the Hippodrome, across the main street from the Augoustaion and near the imperial palace.[161] According to a tradition which first appears in the sixth century in the Chronicle of Ioannes Malalas, the building was begun in the age of the Roman emperor Septimius Severus (193–211), but left unfinished. Under Constantine it was finally completed, decorated with ancient statues and inaugurated together with the new city in 330. Shortly after 500, the poet Christodoros of Koptos described these statues in an *ekphrasis*. During the Nika Riots in 532, the Zeuxippos baths burned down, the statues were probably destroyed and were not replaced when the building was restored thereafter.

The baths were still in operation until the early eighth century, but then fell into disrepair, were used for other purposes, and finally disappeared completely. A small part of them was excavated in 1928/29, revealing that the bath proper was attached to a big peristyle courtyard – probably the place where the statues had once stood. The evidence seemed to suggest that the first phase of the building actually predated the age of Constantine;[162] more recent investigations, however, have shown that no building stood on the site before him.[163] During the excavation, three statue bases were found – two of them inscribed – and parts of a colossal female marble head.

Until today, most authors assume that the statues of the Zeuxippos were all set up under Constantine and formed a coherent ensemble. But this is hard to believe: we know that honorary statues of officials were occasionally being placed there in the late fifth century,[164] and of the three bases found during excavation of the baths, two were already reused, and their cylindrical shape suggests that they post-date Constantine's age.

Our only detailed source for the statues of the Zeuxippos is the *ekphrasis* by Christodoros of Koptos, a poem of 416 hexametrical verses that describes eighty-one statues or statue groups of gods, demigods, mythological figures and historical persons. Some descriptions allow us to recognise certain iconographical types of ancient art, such as Hermes solving his sandals,[165] the naked

---

[161] On this collection see, among others, Stupperich, 'Statuenprogramm'; Guberti Bassett, 'Historiae custos'; Tissoni, *Cristodoro*; Bassett, *Urban Image*, pp. 160–85; Kaldellis, 'Christodoros'; Croke, 'Poetry'; Bär, 'Museum of words'; Martins de Jesus, 'Statuary collection'; Whitby, 'Christodorus'; Saradi, 'Christodorus'.

[162] Casson et al., *Preliminary Report*.

[163] Puech, 'Statues', quoting Pont, Pont, 'Septime Sévère', pp. 194–6.

[164] In 467: Ioannes Malalas 14.38.

[165] Von Mosch, 'Sandalenlöser', assumed that this was the original statue created by Lysippos and originally endowed to the sanctuary of Muses at the Helicon in 338 BC.

Achilleus and the semi-nude Aphrodite. Many others, however, are not easy to understand since the emphasis of this rhetorical text lies more in the depiction of the emotions and experiences of the portrayed persons than of their outer appearance. Repeatedly, the poet insists that bronze is mute and therefore cannot fully represent the depicted persons, and that it is his task to supply by his words what is missing.[166] The meaning of the collection as a whole, if there was one, is also not clearly given, and its analysis is hampered by the fact that the poem is obviously incomplete.[167]

Of the eighty-one statues, twenty-nine show persons connected to the Trojan war and especially to the conquest of Troy. In a seminal study, Reinhard Stupperich suggested in 1982 that the poem propagates the idea of Constantinople as the new Troy. But the well-known legend that Constantine restored rightful rule over the world (that of the Trojans) to the place where it belonged, by founding his new city in the east, is not attested before the sixth century, and contrary to what Stupperich assumed, there is no trace of it in Constantine's own era. The legend made sense only after the end of the western Roman empire in 476, and gained importance only in the age of Justinian, when the reconquest of Italy from the Ostrogoths made it necessary to explain why the emperor stayed in Constantinople and did not return to old Rome.

Christodoros' poem is, in fact, the first place where the legend is attested. The statues depicting persons from the Trojan war must either have been set up in the Zeuxippos baths long after Constantine – perhaps shortly before the poem was written – or Christodoros identified as such other, uninscribed statues that had been standing there for a long time. In fact, some of the Trojans mentioned are rather obscure figures, and no iconography of them is known.

If we look on the other statues, we realise that Christodoros' identification of persons does not always match their known iconography, and in more than one case he himself expresses doubts about the identity of a person:[168]

> There stood one named Alkmaion the prophet; but he was not the famous prophet, nor wore the laurel berries on his hair. I conjecture he was Alkman, who formerly practised the lyric art, weaving a Doric song on his sweet-toned strings.

The historical persons in this collection have nothing to do with Byzantium and Constantinople, with only one exception: Pompeios, the well-known Roman general of the late republican age, who had become famous for his successful

---

[166] Kaldellis, 'Christodoros', p. 363.
[167] It clearly lacks an introduction, but the end is complete, see Kaldellis, 'Christodoros', pp. 377–8.
[168] *Anthologia graeca*, 2.393–7.

wars against the Cilician pirates of his time, was claimed by the propaganda of Anastasios as his ancestor after the successful war against the Isaurians – that the Isaurians lived in roughly the same geographical area had helped support his claim. Christodoros himself wrote a now lost poem about this war, and in the *ekphrasis* of the Zeuxippos bath, looking at a statue in the bath, he draws a close parallel between Anastasios and Pompeios:[169]

> Pompeios, the leader of the successful Romans in their campaign against the Isaurians, was treading under foot the Isaurian swords, signifying that he had imposed on the neck of Taurus the yoke of bondage, and bound it with the strong chains of victory. He was the man who was a light to all and the father of the noble race of the Emperor Anastasios. This my excellent Emperor showed to all, himself vanquishing by his arms the inhabitants of Isauria.

Anastasios himself had a nephew called Pompeios who held the consulate in 501 and may well have ordered Christodoros' poem. There is every reason to assume, therefore, that many of the statues in the Zeuxippos bath were set up there not long before this time, and that most of them were reused and renamed pieces.

16.3 The Palace of Lausos

Lausos, eunuch and imperial chamberlain in the age of Theodosios II, built a palace on the Mese around 420 that housed a famous collection of ancient statues.[170] This collection is described twice in the chronicle of Georgios Kedrenos, again a paraphrase of a poem by Constantine of Rhodes. The first description is in the section on the monuments of Constantinople at the end of the reign of Theodosios I in 395, the second in the report about the destruction of this palace by fire in 475; I quote here the first instance:[171]

> There stood also a statue of Lindian Athena, four cubits high, of emerald stone, the work of the sculptors Skyllis and Dipoinos, which once upon a time Sesostris, tyrant of Egypt, sent as a gift to Kleoboulos, tyrant of Lindos. Likewise the Knidian Aphrodite of white stone, naked, shielding with her hand only her pudenda, a work of Praxiteles of Knidos. Also the Samian Hera, a work of Lysippos and the Chian Boupalos; a winged Eros holding a bow, brought from Myndos; the ivory Zeus by Phidias, whom Perikles dedicated at the temple of the Olympians; the statue representing Chronos, a work of Lysippos, bald at the back and having hair in front; unicorns, tigresses, vultures, giraffes, a buffalo, centaurs and pans.

[169] Ibid., 2.398–404.
[170] Mango et al., 'Palace of Lausus'; Bardill, 'Palace of Lausus'; Bassett, 'Excellent offerings', and 'Curious art', pp. 250–7.
[171] Georgios Kedrenos, c. 344.6.

We do not know upon which source Constantine of Rhodes' lost poem was based, but it is clear there is some confusion: Sesostris is called Amasis in Kedrenos' second, and later, description; he is the Egyptian king mentioned by Herodotos as dedicating a statue of Athena at Lindos,[172] but no ancient text ascribes this statue to the famous sculptors Skyllis and Dipoinos. The Knidian Aphrodite is described correctly and known from many surviving copies, but Praxiteles should be from Athens, not from Knidos. Lysippos lived in the fourth century BC, two hundred years after Boupalos; his name is probably misplaced and actually belongs to the statue of Eros stringing the bow, which is usually attributed to him and also known from many copies. The Samian Hera, then, would have been ascribed to Boupalos alone in the lost source of the poem, since its sculptor, the legendary Smilis, was unknown to its author.[173] The ivory Zeus of Olympia, a work of Phidias from about 435 BC, is often mentioned and described by ancient texts. It showed the god sitting on a throne, half naked, with a statuette of Nike in one hand and a sceptre in the other. The statue was 30 ells or 13.5 metres high, and consisted of ivory plates and gilded panels on a wooden framework. Chronos, the god of time, is also attested by some sources in the way described above as a work of Lysippos.

All in all, the list makes the impression that Constantine's poem was based on a good ancient source, though probably not on the lost fifth-century history of Malchos; this is what an addition to a quote from Kedrenos in the twelfth-century chronicle of Ioannes Zonaras says.[174]

Of all these statues, at least the Lindian Athena and the Zeus from Olympia are described in a way which suggests that they were ancient Greek originals. Only the last part with animals and mythological figures, which is missing in the second description, was probably inspired by the author's own imagination.

17 Statues in the Hippodrome

Following the tradition of the *Circus maximus* in Rome and its many copies in the Roman provinces, the Hippodrome of Constantinople was decorated with numerous statues on the so-called *spina*, the long and low separating wall along the longitudinal axis of the racecourse, which was here divided into a number of sections separated by passageways.[175] Traditionally, the most important monument of the *spina* was an obelisk. Since a real Egyptian obelisk was not easy to obtain, the Hippodrome of Constantinople first received an imitation obelisk of masonry with a revetment of gilded bronze plates, and only later, in 392, a real obelisk from Thebes.[176]

---

[172] Herodotos, 2.182. [173] Frickenhaus, 'Eros'.
[174] Ioannes Zonaras, vol. 3, pp. 130.15–131.12. [175] Dagron, 'L'organisation', pp. 102–24.
[176] Effenberger, 'Überlegungen'.

The statues of the Hippodrome are occasionally mentioned by the sources, but never in a systematic survey. A considerable number of them is described by the *Parastaseis*, but the information given there is gathered from very disparate sources of different age, and it is obviously incomplete. The *Patria* reproduce the *Parastaseis* in a more systematic arrangement, but with only few substantial additions.

When the Crusaders of the Fourth Crusade conquered and sacked Constantinople in 1204, most ancient statues in the Hippodrome and elsewhere in the city were destroyed. The historian Niketas Choniates bewails this event in his famous text *On the Statues*, which was written in exile in Asia Minor. *On the Statues* is a brilliant work of literature and a fascinating witness to the author's esteem and admiration for the works of ancient Greek art. But like the previous texts, it does not intend to give a complete survey of these statues; the descriptions do not always match the known ancient iconography, and although Niketas certainly saw these statues himself before their destruction, the information about them often comes from literary sources. In Niketas' perception, the reason for this unprecedented act of vandalism was simply the Crusader's greed for money:[177]

> Because they were in want of money – for the barbarians are unable to sate their love of riches –, they covetously eyed the bronze statues and consigned these to the flames.

The reality is probably different, for the statues of the Hippodrome were, without doubt, perceived by the Crusaders as magical objects which bore in themselves the strength of the Byzantine empire, and had therefore to be destroyed.[178]

The overlap between the *Parastaseis* and Niketas Choniates seems small at first sight, for not more than three statues or groups of statues are clearly described by both the *Parastaseis* and Niketas. These merit a more detailed presentation:

17.1 The Skylla

The Skylla group was already on display in the Hippodrome in the fourth century.[179] In the early sixth century, two satirical epigrams on the avarice of the Emperor Anastasios I suggest that his statue stood close to it:[180]

---

[177] Niketas Choniates, p. 648.35–7.
[178] See the remarks by Robert de Clari in Section 17.7 below.
[179] It is mentioned in a Latin poem, probably translated from Greek, which is preserved in a collection from ca. 400 AD – see *Epigrammata Bobiensia*, no. 51 – and may also be the Skylla in Themistios' *Oration* 22, 279b; cf. Cameron, *Porphyrius*, p. 185 with note 3. Andreae and Conticello, 'Skylla und Charybdis', p. 42 f. propose, in contrast, that the group was brought to Constantinople only after 515 AD.
[180] *Anthologia graeca*, 11.270 and 271.

Emperor, destroyer of the world, they set up this iron statue for you as being much less precious than bronze, in return for the bloodshed, the fatal poverty and famine and wrath, by which thou destroy all things by your avarice.

Near to Skylla they set up cruel Charybdis, this savage man-eater Anastasios. Fear it in your heart, Skylla, lest he devour you too, turning a bronze goddess into small change.

The Skylla is described in detail only in Niketas Choniates' *Book of the Statues* on the occasion of its destruction by the crusaders in 1204. Niketas says:

The ancient Skylla is depicted leaning forward as she leaped into Odysseus's ships and devoured many of his companions: in female form down to the waist, huge-breasted and full of savagery, and below the waist divided into beasts of prey.[181]

This suggests that the monument, probably a work of the Hellenistic period, was similar to the well-known Skylla group found at Sperlonga in Italy, which may in fact be a copy of it.[182] The *Parastaseis* clearly speak about the same object, though without identifying it as a Skylla, and explain it as an oracle:[183]

Among the female statues, that near the epigram of the Medes is of women giving birth to wild beasts and devouring men. One of them, Herodianos made clear to me, reveals the story of the godless Justinian. The other, which is accompanied also by a boat, has not been fulfilled, but remains.

The first part of this oracle, as we see, refers to the evil deeds of Emperor Justinian II (685–95 and 705–11) and had already been fulfilled when the *Parastaseis* was written. But what about the second part? When the entry was taken over into the *Patria*, the redactor changed the end as follows:[184]

... which is accompanied also by a boat, is, according to some, Skylla who devours the men thrown out by Charybdis, and it is Odysseus whom she holds with her hand by his head. Others say that this is earth, the sea and the seven ages of the world which are devoured by the floods, and the present age is the seventh one.

Here, the correct identification as a Skylla has been given, but is combined with a new interpretation, for at the end of the world, according to the apocalyptic texts, Constantinople will be drowned in the sea.[185]

[181] Niketas Choniates, p. 651.27–31.
[182] See, among others, Andreae and Conticello, 'Skylla und Charybdis', pp. 25–6.
[183] *Parastaseis*, c. 61, with notes in Cameron and Herrin, *Constantinople*, p. 250f. See also Dagron, *Constantinople imaginaire*, pp. 147–9.
[184] *Patria*, 279.   [185] See, for example, Berger, 'Konstantinopel', pp. 142–4.

Figure 11 *The Skylla group from Sperlonga.*
Credit: N. Himmelmann, *Sperlonga*: *Die homerischen Gruppen und ihre Bildquellen* (Opladen 1996), plate 8 on p. 82.

In the end the Skylla group suffered the fate which had been prophesied seven hundred years earlier in the epigram on Anastasios: as Niketas Choniates reports, it was melted down by the crusaders and cut up into small coin.

17.2 The 'bath attendant'

The *Parastaseis* contain a long and strange chapter in which Emperor Theodosios II (408–50) discusses the statues of the Hippodrome with seven pagan philosophers from Athens. At the end of it, the statue of a man is mentioned who is dressed only in a loincloth, has a helmet on his head and is driving a donkey; one of the philosophers, Kranos by name, says: 'One day a donkey will be like a man; what a fate for a man to follow a donkey!'

The *Patria*, when retelling this story, call the statue the 'bath attendant' because of its dress. But what was its real meaning? When describing the same object, Niketas Choniates tells us that it had once been set up at Aktion by Emperor Augustus to commemorate his victory in the Roman civil war in 31 BC, for the following reason:

> When he went out by night to inspect the army of Antonius, he met a man driving a donkey, and when he asked him who he was and where he went, he was told: 'My name is Nikon and my donkey is called Nikandros, and I am going to Caesar's camp.'

This story is taken from Plutarch's *Life of Antonius*[186] where, however, the man is called Eutychos and the donkey Nikon – and there is no way to tell whether the 'bath attendant' really commemorated this event in Roman history or not.

17.3 Hippopotamus vs. crocodile

Supported by the authority of Philip the dynast, a fictitious person, the *Parastaseis* asserts:[187]

> While the dragon statue is a representation of Arkadios, it is a display of his brother Honorios, reigning in Rome. Not a few oracles have taken place there, both before our time and up to the present day.

It is difficult to understand this entry, for the sense of the words *ektypoma* and *epideixis*, which are rendered here as 'representation' and 'display', is not entirely clear. The artwork may have shown either one or two animals of which at least one was a dragon, i.e., that it was covered by scales or osteoderms and had legs. The only object, which can possibly be identified with it, is this group described by Niketas Choniates at the end of his *On the Statues*:[188]

> A delight to behold and almost more wondrous in craftsmanship than all the others was the bronze animal standing on a stone pedestal. It did not portray an unambiguous bull for it was short-tailed and neither had a thick throat such as the Egyptian bulls have, nor was it equipped with cloven hooves. In its jaws it throttled another animal whose body was covered all over with scales so prickly that even in bronze it caused pain to him who touched them. This animal, clenched in the bull's mouth, appeared to some to be a basilisk and to others an asp; not a few conjectured that the one was a Nile bull and the other a crocodile.

---

[186] *Life of Antonius*, 65.2.   [187] *Parastaseis*, c. 62.
[188] Niketas Choniates, pp. 653.27–655.65.

The last conjecture is, of course, correct: the fight between a hippopotamus and a crocodile is a well-known motif of ancient Egyptian art, which can be found on cameos and other art work from the Roman age,[189] and the object in the Hippodrome was apparently a monumental, three-dimensional version of it.

Niketas then describes, in lively words and great detail, the struggle between the two animals which finally kill each other, and thus represent, in an allegorical way, the Crusaders who will, as he hopes, find the same end:

> This mutual destruction and killing has persuaded me to say that these death-dealing evils, ruinous to men, not only are portrayed in images and not only happen to the bravest of beasts, but frequently occur among the nations, such as those which have marched against us Romans, killing and being killed, perishing by the of Christ who scatters those nations which wish for wars and who does not rejoice in bloodshed, and who causes the just man to tread on the asp and the basilisk and to trample under foot the lion and the dragon.

In this way the group becomes an allegory of the Crusaders and gains a new meaning in the direct context of the Crusader's conquest in 1204.[190] If the identification of this group with the dragon of the *Parastaseis* is correct, the entry there suggests that the two brothers Honorios (395–423) and Arkadios (395–408) were hostile to each other. It is true that their respective governments often acted against each other in the thirteen years of their simultaneous rule, but there was no official war, and nothing is known about the personal relationship of the brothers.

17.4 The boar of bronze and Herakles

Despite some stories about their magical powers, the nude statues in the Hippodrome were mostly simply accepted as works of ancient art, and almost no moral censure of them was expressed. It is an exception, therefore, if we read in the tenth-century *Life of Saint Andrew the Fool* that a woman suffered the disturbing dream that she stood in the Hippodrome, embracing the statues and feeling an impure desire to have intercourse with them.[191]

The active use of statues in the Hippodrome for magical practices begins, according to our sources, in the time of Emperor Alexandros, the younger brother and co-emperor of Leon VI. Alexandros reigned alone after Leon's death for one year from 912 to 913, and little has remained of him except the beautiful mosaic portrait on the northern gallery of Hagia Sophia. His reputation in the sources was that of an elderly debauchee, who was inhibited from doing

---

[189] Pingitzer, 'Nilpferd'.　　[190] Papamastorakis, 'Interpreting', pp. 215–7.
[191] *Life of Andrew the Fool*, line 2492 with note 10 on p. 332; Mango, 'Antique statuary', pp. 59–62.

grave damage to the state only by his early death. The Continuation of Theophanes tells us this story:[192]

> This Alexandros put his trust in deceivers and wizards and was convinced by them that the bronze wild boar standing in the Hippodrome was his magic statue. They pointed out that he was in competition with Leon his brother, thus showing that this foolish man was piggish. Deceived by them, he provided the pig with the genitals and tusks it lacked.

This boar is not mentioned in the *Parastaseis* or *Patria*. It stood, as it seems, near the statue of a lion, and played a role in magical practices about three hundred years later. But let us first go on with the text of the Continuation of Theophanes:

> While he was prey to such a deceit, he arranged chariot races, took the holy tapestries and candelabra from the churches and decorated the Hippodrome, thus offering God's honour to idols in his vileness. Therefore his honour was also very quickly taken away by God.

This imputation, at least, is much older than the Continuation of Theophanes: Alexandros had removed the patriarch Euthymios from office in 912, and when Euthymios died in exile in 917, the well-known intellectual Arethas of Caesarea held a funeral oration in which he claimed that Alexandros had sacrificed to the statues of the Hippodrome at the *Anthesteria*, an ancient spring feast of Dionysos.[193] And Euthymios' hagiography, written some years later, tells us the actual reason for Alexandros' engagement in magic:

> For now Alexandros, the emperor, hindered of his amorous passion, and remaining impotent therein, addressed himself to sorcerers, being led by them to lawless deeds, putting clothes upon the bronze figures of the Zodiac in the Hippodrome, incensing them, and having them illuminated with candelabra.[194]

Is this pure propaganda, or does the story have a real core? And if so, about which statues are we talking? The *Life of Euthymios* identifies them, rightly or wrongly, as a representation of the Zodiac, which suggests that they were a group of twelve.

Recently, Robert Coates-Stephens has drawn our attention to a Latin chronicle from Salerno in Italy, which was written some decades after these events. It tells the same story, but claims that the statues in question were seventy in number, and that they were brought from the Capitol in Rome only in Alexandros' time. In Rome they had once been set up as a magical device to detect uprisings of the

---

[192] *Theophanes continuatus* (Bekker), p. 379.12–21. Ioannes Skylitzes, pp. 194.80–195.89 has a slightly expanded version.
[193] Arethas, 'Funeral oration', p. 91.7–9.   [194] *Life of Euthymios*, 12.23–9.

subdued peoples.[195] This so-called *salvatio Romae* legend was quite popular in the west, but only the Salerno chronicle connects it to statues at a place other than Rome. Coates-Stephens suggests that the legend is, in fact, of Constantinopolitan origin and may have been inspired by a group of statues in the Hippodrome – which may have, in turn, once been brought from Rome, of course long before Alexandros. Ancient sources mention some statues in Rome showing personifications of peoples and cities that would be ideal candidates for Coates-Stephens' suggestion. A reused inscription in Old St. Peter's has been identified as the Trajanic dedication of the *Porticus Divorum*. Coates-Stephens proposes, therefore, that the gallery of Caesars was, in fact, dismantled under Constantine, and would therefore have been available for the decoration of Constantinople. We would then have another case in which statues were removed of their pagan religious context in Rome, only to be set up in a similar pagan or semi-pagan context in Constantinople again.

Unfortunately, this is all hypothetical, and Coates-Stephens clearly errs, at least in the end, when connecting to this story in a Latin chronicle a list in the *Patria* of cities from which the statues in the Hippodrome had been brought.[196] This list was added at the last redaction of the *Patria* in 989/90 and contains only places that then belonged, still or again, to the Byzantine empire.[197]

But let us return to the bronze boar: shortly before Constantinople was taken by the Crusaders in 1204 and most of its statues were destroyed, the Empress Euphrosyne, wife of Alexios III Angelos, used it again for magical practices, as Niketas Choniates reports:[198]

> In her predictions of the things to come, she devoted herself to unspeakable rituals and divinations and practised many abominable rites. She went so far as to cut off the snout of the bronze Kalydonian boar which stands in the Hippodrome with its back bristling and advances with projecting tusks against a lion, and she conceived of having the back of the gloriously triumphant Herakles, Lysimachos' most beautiful work, in which the hero holds his head in his hand and bewails his fate while a lion's skin is spread out over a basket, lacerated by repeated flogging.

Euphrosyne, it seems, let the boar be mutilated in the hope of keeping the 'swinish and reckless populace' of Constantinople under control. This is the expression used by Niketas Choniates several pages later, when he describes how the boar was removed from the Hippodrome to the Great Palace, shortly before the city was finally taken and plundered.[199] It is also Niketas Choniates who identifies the statue as the Kalydonian boar from the ancient myth of Herakles.

[195] Coates-Stephens, 'Byzantine Sack'.   [196] *Patria*, 2.73.
[197] Berger, *Untersuchungen*, p. 544.   [198] Niketas Choniates, p. 519.44–51.
[199] Ibid., p. 558.41–6.

Figure 12 Herakles on an ivory casket.
Credit: Photograph courtesy of Stephan Kube, StiftsMuseum Xanten.

The statue of Herakles is described twice in Niketas' work, here and, in much more detail, in *On the Statues* where he says:[200]

> The statue was so large that it took a cord the size of a man's belt to go round the thumb, and the shin was the size of a man.

If this is correct, then the statue was at least four times larger than life. Niketas calls it a work of Lysimachos both times which is certainly an error for Lysippos. The statue is also mentioned in other Byzantine sources,[201] and replicas and depictions of it can be identified in some ancient and medieval objects of art, with the closest iconographical parallel being on an ivory casket now in Xanten in Germany.[202] *On the Statues* also mentions a man wrestling

---

[200] Ibid., pp. 649.84–650.9.

[201] Constantine Porphyrogennetos, *De thematibus*, 87.14–16; Konstantinos Manasses, *Ekphrasis*, line 18–22.

[202] Bassett, *Urban Image*, pp. 152–4; Mathiopulu, 'Klassisches und Klassizistisches', pp. 36–9; Floren, 'Lysipps Statuen'.

with a lion; this must have been another statue of Herakles, this time fighting the Nemean lion, but is not identified as such.[203]

17.5 Emperors, pagan gods, and animals

The statues of the Hippodrome, which are described by the *Parastaseis* and the *Patria*, often cannot be identified easily.

Since the *Parastaseis* are, as mentioned before, compiled from different sources, their text also contains a number of doublets. A good example is the monumental statue of Herakles, whose correct name the *Parastaseis* know only in the context of its alleged first place of display, the Basilica:[204] in the Hippodrome, the same statue is mentioned without its name as 'in the south', and another time as 'the big statue in the Hippodrome which holds its hand before the face'.[205] It may even be identical with the crooked statue of Emperor Diocletian from Nikomedeia, and with the statue of Zeus from Ikonion.[206]

Another case: at a place called the Youth (Neolaia), which must have been in or near the Hippodrome, the *Parastaseis* describe the statues of a woman on a chariot and an altar with a calf, and four gilded horses and a chariot with a charioteer who holds a running female statue in his hand.[207] This is clearly the group we have discussed in Section 5 above, to which the horses of San Marco had once belonged – but it is described here in the state *before* it was dispersed and partially destroyed, an event which must have happened by the mid-fourth century. Later in the same text, however, the same four horses are mentioned alone, and Chios is said to be their place of origin.[208]

A number of other statues are mentioned only in the *Parastaseis*, such as the equestrian statue of Emperor Justinian in the Kathisma – the imperial lodge of the Hippodrome – which may be the same as the riding emperor some chapters later,[209] and the uninscribed Augustus from Rome. Rare are the cases such as the following one in which an ancient statue is explained as a person of Byzantine history:[210]

> The statue seated on a bronze chair is, as Herodian says, Verina, the wife of Leo the Great. Others say that this is Athene which came from Greece. And this I believed.

---

[203] Niketas Choniates, p. 650.20.   [204] See Section 17.4 above.
[205] *Parastaseis*, c. 64 and 65.   [206] *Parastaseis*, c. 76 and 83; the former also *Patria*, 2.73.
[207] *Parastaseis*, c. 5.   [208] Ibid., c. 84.   [209] Ibid., c. 61 and 64; the latter also *Patria*, 2.82.
[210] *Parastaseis*, c. 61; *Patria*, 2.78. This may also be the female figure inscribed in the zodiac signs in *Parastaseis*, c. 64; *Patria*, 2.82.

In an entry of the *Patria*, the identification of a bronze statue as Empress Eirene (797–802) can be simply excluded by the fact that this empress and her son Constantine VI (780–97) lived at a time when the technique of hollow casting was lost:[211]

> The female statue of bronze on the small column in the fountain basin of the Hippodrome is Eirene the Athenian. Her son Constantine set it up for her disport.

17.6 Niketas Choniates and the statues of the Hippodrome

Our final source for the statues of Constantinople is *On the Statues* by Niketas in which he describes how most of them were destroyed by the Crusaders of the Fourth Crusade in 1204, both in the Hippodrome and elsewhere in the city. Niketas lists and describes a number of statues which are unknown to the *Parastaseis* and *Patria*, and have therefore not been discussed yet.

Niketas begins with detailed reports about the destruction of the Hera at the forum, the Anemodoulion, the rider of the Tauros, the monumental Herakles in the Hippodrome and the donkey with its driver.[212] He then lists a hyena, a she-wolf suckling Romulus and Remus and a man wrestling with a lion;[213] then a number of animal statues, such as sphinxes, a hippopotamus, an elephant and an unbridled horse, and, with some description, the Skylla.[214] The following sections are more detailed again, describing a bronze eagle with a snake in its claws, beautiful Helena, a young woman holding in her palm a man on a horse, and statues of victorious charioteers, before the text ends with a long allegorical interpretation of the group of hippopotamus and crocodile.[215]

Let us begin with remarks about some of the objects which are listed by Niketas only shortly: the hyena is already mentioned in the *Parastaseis* with Antioch as its place of origin,[216] while the she-wolf appears only here. Niketas seems to say that one of them had suckled Romulus, the other Remus. But such a legend is unknown, and we would rather expect only a she-wolf suckling both boys, such as in the well-known Capitoline Wolf in Rome.[217] Niketas, however, clearly distinguishes both statues at a previous mention,[218] and does not say that Romulus and Remus were actually depicted.

---

[211] *Patria*, 3.202.   [212] Niketas Choniates, pp. 648.38–650.16; see above p. 25, 27, and 50.
[213] Niketas Choniates, p. 650.17–20; on the wrestling man, see Sections 4.7 and 17 above.
[214] Niketas Choniates, pp. 650.20–651.31; on the Skylla, see Section 17.1 above.
[215] See Section 17.3 above.   [216] *Parastaseis*, c. 62; *Patria*, 2.79.
[217] Recent research has shown that this statue is probably not of Etruscan origin as hitherto assumed, but was cast in the eleventh or twelfth century, with the twins Romulus and Remus added in the fifteenth century.
[218] Niketas Choniates, p. 350.37–8.

The statue of a young woman with the rider in her hand and the charioteers stood next to each other 'very close to the eastern turn of the four-horse chariot course called the Red', that is, in the northeastern part of the Hippodrome.[219] The statues of charioteers were set up in the sixth century on high pillars. They had verse inscriptions which have been preserved in *The Greek Anthology*, and two of the pillars have been found, without the statues, at excavations.[220]

The two important remaining objects in Niketas' report require a more detailed discussion. The description of the bronze eagle begins with these words: [221]

> There was set up in the Hippodrome a bronze eagle, the novel device of Apollonios of Tyana, a brilliant instrument of his magic. Once, while visiting among the Byzantines, he was entreated to bring them relief from the snake bites that plagued them. Resorting to those lewd rituals whose celebrants are the demons and all those who pay special honor to their secret rites, he set up on a column an eagle.

The eagle had its wings, as Niketas then says, outspread and held a venomous serpent in its claws. The wings were marked with the hours of the day, so that the statue served also as a sundial 'to those who looked upon it with understanding'.

The installation of statues with magical powers in Constantinople had been attributed to Apollonios of Tyana in the sixth century, as mentioned at the beginning.[222] Niketas mentions him only here, and connects him to an otherwise unknown statue in the Hippodrome, claiming that this statue kept the serpents away from the city.

The description of the statue of Helena, which was also destroyed by the Crusaders, is most remarkable for its strong emotionality:[223]

> What of the white-armed, beautiful-ankled, and long-necked Helen, who mustered the entire host of the Hellenes and overthrew Troy, whence she sailed to the Nile and, after a long absence, returned to the abodes of the Laconians? Was she able to placate the implacable? Was she able to soften those men whose hearts were made of iron? On the contrary! She who had enslaved every onlooker with her beauty was wholly unable to achieve this, even though she was appareled ornately; though fashioned of bronze, she appeared as fresh as the morning dew, anointed with the moistness of erotic love on her garment, veil, diadem, and braid of hair. Her vesture was finer than spider webs, and the veil was cunningly wrought in its place; the diadem of gold and precious stones which bound the forehead was radiant, and the braid of hair that extended down to her knees,

---

[219] Niketas Choniates, p. 653.5–25.   [220] Cameron, *Porphyrius*.
[221] Niketas Choniates, p. 651.32–57.   [222] See Section 1 above.
[223] Niketas Choniates, pp. 652.1–653.25.

flowing down and blowing in the breeze, was bound tightly in the back with a hair band. The lips were like flower cups, slightly parted as though she were about to speak; the graceful smile, at once greeting the spectator, filled him with delight; her flashing eyes, her arched eyebrows, and the shapeliness of the rest of her body were such that they cannot be described in words and depicted for future generations.

Niketas then goes on to declare that the destruction of this statue was an act of revenge against the woman who once had caused the destruction of Troy. But his description does not allow us to identify the statue with any known icono-graphical type of antiquity. Also, there are no recorded examples for statues of Helena, and Niketas probably described a statue of Aphrodite instead. But as Titos Papamastorakis has pointed out, this was no error or misunderstanding: Niketas intentionally attached this new identification to the statue in order to give a symbolic interpretation to it, and to connect it to the Crusader's attack on Constantinople.[224]

17.7 The apocalyptical Hippodrome

The fear of the approaching end of the world is a constant motif of popular literature in Byzantium, and many were the attempts to predict its exact time.[225] Also, there was a firm belief that ancient statues and inscriptions contained prophecies about it, and the statues in the Hippodrome lent them-selves perfectly to this idea. The list of statues in the Hippodrome in the *Parastaseis*, for example, is taken over by the *Patria* with this additional remark at the end:[226]

> Various statues were brought by Constantine the Great which were also set up and upon which spells were cast. Whoever passes by them and understands them will clearly understand from them the final destiny.

And a bit further on:[227]

> The remaining statues of the Hippodrome, the men and women, the various horses, the columns of stone and bronze and the bronze obelisks at the turning points, the representations on the obelisk, the statues of the charioteers with their bases in relief, the columns of the galleries with their capitals and pedestals and those in the curved part, the marble revetments and reliefs, the steps and podia and every place where an inscription can be found, especially on the bronze statues – all these are representations of the last days and the future. Apollonios set them up here in memory of the events, in

---

[224] Papamastorakis, 'Interpreting', pp. 220–2.
[225] See, among others, Magdalino, 'End of time', with the bibliography given there.
[226] *Patria*, 2.73.   [227] Ibid., 2.79.

order to make them immortal, and he also cast spells on the statues in the entire city. Whoever has any experience of the representations of fate will discover everything clearly. The Delphic tripods with the bowls and the statues on horseback also bear inscriptions as to why they were set up and what they mean.

In this text, Apollonios of Tyana is not only, as in older texts and also in Niketas Choniates, a good magician who protects the city by his spells. Here, he has finally become the master of all magic and prophet of the city's future, a role which is assigned in later times to Leon the Wise, that is, to Emperor Leon VI (886–912).[228]

Regarding the Hippodrome, the final stage of the legend is reached in Robert de Clari's account about the conquest of Constantinople in 1204, which tells us that all the statues in the Hippodrome had once been alive and had taken part in the games.[229]

18 The Statues of Constantinople in the Late Byzantine Age

After 1204 all major ancient bronze statues of Constantinople were destroyed except the rider of Justinian on the column near Hagia Sophia. In the Hippodrome, there were still the two obelisks, the Egyptian one and the one of masonry, and as the only major object of bronze the Serpent column which stood between them. A statue of a goose, which may have belonged to a fountain, is the only object of bronze from the Byzantine age that has been found in the Hippodrome.[230]

The Serpent column consists of three snakes with their bodies twined together, and heads looking in different directions.[231] It once supported a monumental tripod offered by the Greek cities after their victory over the Persians at Plataiai in 479 BC. The tripod was already lost by the time of the Romans, and there is no information about when the column was brought to Constantinople. We should assume that this happened in Constantine's age or shortly thereafter, but there is no clear mention of it, at the Hippodrome or elsewhere, before the late fourteenth century. It is probable that the Serpent column was set up in the Hippodrome only at some point after the Byzantine reconquest of the city in 1261. In this period, it seems to have functioned as a fountain.[232]

Reports of visitors from the late fourteenth and fifteenth centuries show that it was the only remarkable object of bronze which had remained in the Hippodrome, and it is not surprising that all sorts of legends were now associated with it.[233] The belief in its magical power to keep snakes away from the city was so strong that it survived even the Ottoman conquest of the city in 1453 and

---

[228] Brokkaar, *Oracles*.   [229] Robert de Clari, pp. 109–10.   [230] Loverance, 'Bronze goose'.
[231] Stephenson, *Serpent Column*.   [232] Stephenson, 'Serpent Column fountain'.
[233] Majeska, *Russian Travelers*, pp. 250–8; Griebeler, 'Serpent Column'.

persisted for a long time thereafter: the column stood almost undamaged until it lost the three serpents' heads in the year 1700.[234]

The last Byzantine text, in which the statues of Constantinople are mentioned, is the 'Comparison of old and new Rome', which Manuel Chrysoloras wrote, styled as a letter, to Emperor Manuel II Palaiologos in 1411. Chrysoloras says that formerly there had been many *stelai* and *andriantes* in the city, but that mostly only their bases remained – especially in the Hippodrome. Only the statue of the 'lawgiver', i.e., Justinian on the Augoustaion square, and several others on columns east of it are described as still existing. Chrysoloras also claims that once embossed silver statues of Theodosios I and Theodosios II had stood on the big columns on the Xerolophos and Tauros, and that also the columns on the 'other hill above the house where you now live' and the one near the Church of the Apostles had supported statues. These two columns can be identified with that of Justin II at the Deuteron and that of Michael VIII Palaiologos.[235] What he says about Constantine's column on the forum shows that he was not even aware that a statue had ever stood on it:[236]

> What should I say about the column of porphyry on the same square which raises the cross to a very great height in the courtyard of the palace of Constantine, who set up and established all statues, but defeated all (pagan) images?

Chrysoloras later mentions porphyry statues sitting on thrones and a reclining statue of marble, which can be identified as the 'righteous judges' and the reclining Herakles of *ta Amastrianou*.[237] Also, he tries to give an explanation why the number of statues was so small in Constantinople:

> The reason why there are not more of them is that that city was founded when these things were neglected here by reason of piety, for the people tried to avoid, I think, the similarity with wooden images and idols. How should they have made objects which had been taken down here already before? They made and invented other things, I mean on boards and icons, by painting and mosaic.

This is the only time in the 1,200 years of Byzantine history that such thoughts about the development of art from ancient to medieval have been expressed. When Chrysoloras wrote his 'Comparison of old and new Rome', Constantinople was no longer a city of statues. The last scattered pieces, which are mentioned by him, rapidly disappeared when Constantinople was rebuilt as an Islamic capital after the Ottoman conquest of 1453.

---

[234] Stichel, 'Schlangensäule'.   [235] See under Section 3 above.
[236] Manuel Chrysoloras, c. 46–7.   [237] Ibid., c. 48.

Bibliography

1 Sources

Translations are mentioned here only if they are quoted in the text.

Anna Komnene

Annae Comnenae Alexias, ed.
D. R. Reinsch and A. Kambylis, Corpus
Fontium Historiae Byzantinae 40
(Berlin: De Gruyter, 2001)

Anthologia graeca

The Greek Anthology, ed. and trans.
W. R. Paton (London and New York:
Heinemann, 1916–1919)

Arethas, 'Funeral oration'

In Arethas, *Arethae archiepiscopi
Caesariensis Scripta minora* 1, ed.
L. G. Westerink (Leipzig: Teubner,
1968), 83–93

Chronicon paschale

Chronicon paschale, ed. L. Dindorf
(Bonn: Weber, 1832)

Constantine Porphyrogennetos,
De cerimoniis

Constantin VII Porphyrogénète, *Le Livre
des Cérémonies*, ed. G. Dagron and B.
Flusin, Corpus Fontium Historiae
Byzantinae 52 (Paris: ACHCByz 2020)

De thematibus

Costantino Porfirogenito, *De themati-
bus*, ed. A. Pertusi, Studi e Testi 160
(Città del Vaticano: Biblioteca
Apostolica Vaticana, 1952)

Constantine of Rhodes

Constantine of Rhodes, *On
Constantinople and the Church of the
Holy Apostles*, ed. I. Vassis and
L. James (Farnham: Ashgate, 2012)

Epigrammata Bobiensia

Epigrammata Bobiensia, ed. F. Munari
(Rome: Storia e Letteratura, 1955)

Eusebios, *Church History*

Eusebius, *Kirchengeschichte*, ed.
E. Schwartz, Die Griechischen
Christlichen Schriftsteller 9 (Leipzig:
Hinrichs, 1903–8)

Eusebios, *Life of Constantine*

Eusebius, *Über das Leben des Kaisers
Konstantin*, ed. F. Winkelmann, Die
Griechischen Christlichen Schrift-
steller 7.1 (Berlin: Akademie-Verlag,

Bibliography

1974); trans. A. Cameron and S. G. Hall
as Eusebius, *Life of Constantine* (Oxford:
Clarendon Press, 1999)

Georgios Kedrenos   *Georgii Cedreni Historiarum compendium*, ed. L. Tartaglia, Bollettino dei classici, Supplemento 30 (Rome: Accademia Nazionale dei Lincei, 2016)

Hesychios   T. Preger (ed.), 'Hesychii Illustrii origines Constantinopolitanae' in *Scriptores originum Constantinopolitanarum* 1 (Leipzig: Teubner, 1901)

Ioannes Malalas   *Ioannis Malalae Chronographia*, ed. I. Thurn, Corpus Fontium Historiae Byzantinae 35 (Berlin: De Gruyter, 2000); trans. E. Jeffreys, M. Jeffreys, R. Scott et al. as *The Chronicle of John Malalas*, Byzantina Australiensia 4 (Melbourne: Australian Association for Byzantine Studies, 1986)

Ioannes Skylitzes   *Ioannis Scylitzae Synopsis Historiarum*, ed. I. Thurn, Corpus Fontium Historiae Byzantinae 5 (Berlin: De Gruyter, 1978)

Ioannes Zonaras   *Ioannis Zonarae Epitome historiarum* 3, ed. T. Büttner-Wobst (Bonn: Teubner, 1897)

Konstantinos Manasses, *Ekphrasis*   O. Lampsides, 'Der vollständige Text der Ἔκφρασις Γῆς des Konstantinos Manasses', *Jahrbuch der Österreichischen Byzantinistik* 41 (1991), 194–204

Life of Andrew the Fool   *The Life of St. Andrew the Fool*, ed. L. Rydén, Studia Byzantina Upsaliensia 4 (Uppsala: Uppsala University Press, 1995)

Life of Euthymios   *Vita Euthymii patriarchae CP*, ed. P. Karlin-Hayter, Bibliothèque de Byzantion 3 (Brussels: Éditions de Byzantion, 1970)

Manuel Chrysoloras	C. Billò, 'Manuele Crisolora, Confronto tra l'Antica e la Nuova Roma', *Medioevo Greco* 0 (2000), 5–26; trans. C. Smith as 'Manuel Chrysoloras' comparison of old and new Rome' in *Architecture in the Culture of Early Humanism: Ethics, Aesthetics, and Eloquence, 1400–1470* (New York: Oxford University Press, 1992), 199–215
Marcellinus comes	*Chronica minora* 2, ed. T. Mommsen, Monumenta Germaniae Historica, Auctores antiquissimi 11.1 (Berlin: Weidmann, 1894), 37–108
Michael Attaleiates	*Michaelis Attaliatae Historia*, ed. E. Tsolakis, Corpus Fontium Historiae Byzantinae 50 (Athens: Academy, 2011)
Michael Glykas	*Michaelis Glycae Annales*, ed. I. Bekker (Bonn: Weber, 1836)
Nikephoros, *Breviarium*	Nikephoros, Patriarch of Constantinople, *Short history*, ed. C. Mango, Corpus Fontium Historiae Byzantinae 13 (Washington, DC: Dumbarton Oaks, 1990)
Niketas Choniates	*Nicetae Choniatae historia*, ed. J. van Dieten, Corpus Fontium Historiae Byzantinae 11 (Berlin: De Gruyter, 1975); trans. H. Magoulias as *O City of Byzantium, Annals of Niketas Choniates* (Detroit: Wayne State University Press, 1984)
Parastaseis	In Cameron and Herrin, *Constantinople*
Patria	T. Preger (ed.), 'Patria' in *Scriptores originum Constantinopolitanarum* 2 (Leipzig 1907); trans. A Berger as *Accounts of Medieval Constantinople: The Patria*, Dumbarton Oaks Medieval

Library 24 (Cambridge, MA: Harvard
University Press, 2013)

Prokopios, *Buildings*   *Procopii Caesariensis Opera omnia*
3.2, ed. J. Haury (Leipzig: Teubner,
1913); trans H. B. Dewing as
Buildings, The Loeb Classical Library
343 (London: Heinemann, 1961)

Robert de Clari   *The Conquest of Constantinople*, trans. E.
Holmes McNeal, Records of
Civilization, Sources and Studies 23
(New York: Columbia University Press,
1936)

Symeon Logothetes   *Symeonis Magistri et Logothetae
Chronicon*, ed. S. Wahlgren, Corpus
Fontium Historiae Byzantinae 44.1
(Berlin: De Gruyter, 2006)

Theophanes   *Theophanis chronographia* 1, ed. C. de
Boor (Leipzig: Teubner, 1883)

Theophanes continuatus   *Chronographiae quae Theophanis
Continuati nomine fertur Libri I–IV*,
ed. J. Signes and M. Featherstone,
Corpus Fontium Historiae Byzantinae
53 (Berlin: De Gruyter, 2015);
I. Bekker (ed.), Theophanes continuatus (Bonn: Weber, 1838)

Zosimos   Zosime, *Histoire nouvelle*, ed.
F. Paschoud (Paris: Belles Lettres,
1971–89)

2 Literature

Anderson B., 'Classified knowledge: the epistemology of statuary in the
Parastaseis Syntomoi Chronikai', *Byzantine and Modern Greek Studies*
35 (2011), 1–19
'Leo III and the Anemodoulion', *Byzantinische Zeitschrift* 104 (2011), 41–54
Andreae B., and B. Conticello, 'Skylla und Charybdis: Zur Skylla-Gruppe von
Sperlonga', Abhandlungen der Geistes- und Sozialwissenschaftlichen
Klasse, no. 14 (1987)
Asutay-Effenberger N., *Die Landmauer von Konstantinopel – İstanbul*,
Millennium Studies 18 (Berlin: De Gruyter, 2007)

Bär S., 'Museum of words: Christodorus, the art of *ekphrasis* and the epyllic genre' in M. Baumbach, S. Bär (eds.), Brill's Companion to Greek and Latin Epyllion and its Reception (Leiden and Boston: Brill, 2012), 447–71

Bardill J., *Constantine, Divine Emperor of the Christian Golden Age* (Cambridge: Cambridge University Press, 2012)

'The Palace of Lausus and nearby monuments in Constantinople: a topographical study', *American Journal of Archaeology* 101 (1997), 67–95

Bassett S., ' "Curious art": myth, sculpture, and Christian response in the world of Late Antiquity' in H. Leppin, *Antike Mythologie in christlichen Kontexten der Spätantike*, Millennium Studies 54 (Berlin: De Gruyter, 2015), 240–61

'Excellent offerings: the Lausos Collection in Constantinople', *The Art Bulletin* 82 (2000), 6–25

The Urban Image of Late Antique Constantinople (Cambridge: Cambridge University Press, 2004)

Belobrova O. A., 'Статуя византийского императора Юстиниана в древнерусских письменных источниках и иконографии', *Vizantiyskiy Vremmenik* 17 (1960), 114–23

Berger A., 'Das apokalyptische Konstantinopel' in Brandes and Schmieder, *Endzeiten*, 135–55

'Das Haus des Manns aus Amastris: Zu einem Gebäudekomplex im byzantinischen Konstantinopel', *Acta antiqua Academiae Scientiarum Hungaricae* 51 (2011), 87–96

'Tauros e Sigma. Due piazze di Costantinopoli' in *Bisanzio e l'Occidente: Arte, archeologia, storia. Studi in onore di Fernanda de' Maffei* (Rome: Viella, 1996), 17–31

Untersuchungen zu den Patria Konstantinupoleos, Poikila Byzantina 8 (Bonn: Habelt, 1988)

Bianchetti S., *Falaride e Pseudofalaride: storia e leggenda* (Rome: L'Erma di Bretschneider, 1987)

Boeck E. N., *Imagining the Byzantine Past: The perception of History in the Illustrated Manuscripts of Skylitzes and Manasses* (Cambridge: Cambridge University Press, 2015)

The Bronze Horseman of Justinian in Constantinople: The Cross-Cultural Biography of a Mediterranean Monument (Cambridge: Cambridge University Press, 2021)

Brandes W. and F. Schmieder (eds.), *Endzeiten*, Millennium-Studien 16 (Berlin: De Gruyter, 2008)

Brokkaar W. G., *The Oracles of the Most Wise Emperor Leo and the Tale of the True Emperor (Amstelodamensis Graecus VI E 8)* (Amsterdam: Nieuwgriekse Taal- en Letterkunde en Byzantinologie, 2002)

Cameron A., *The Greek Anthology from Meleager to Planudes* (Oxford: Clarendon Press, 1993)

Porphyrius the Charioteer (Oxford: Clarendon Press, 1973)

Cameron A. and J. Herrin, *Constantinople in the Early Eighth Century: The Parastaseis Syntomoi Chronikai (with translation)*, Columbia Studies in the Classical Tradition 10 (Leiden: Brill, 1984)

Casson S., D. Talbot Rice, G. F. Hudson and A. H. M. Jones, *Preliminary Report upon the Excavations Carried out in the Hippodrome of Constantinople in 1927 on Behalf of the British Academy* (London: Milford, 1928)

Chatterjee P., 'Viewing the unknown in eighth-century Constantinople', *Gesta* 56 (2017), 137–49

Coates-Stephens R., 'The Byzantine sack of Rome', *Antiquité Tardive* 25 (2017), 191–212

Croke B., 'Poetry and propaganda: Anastasius I as Pompey', *Greek, Roman and Byzantine Studies* 48 (2008), 447–66

Dagron G., *Constantinople imaginaire. Études sur le reueil des Patria, Bibliothèque byzantine*, Études 8 (Paris: Presses universitaires de France, 1984)

Naissance d'une capitale. Constantinople et ses institutions de 330 à 451, Bibliothèque byzantine 7 (Paris: Presses universitaires de France, 1974)

'L'organisation et le déroulement des courses d'après le Livre de cérémonies', *Travaux et mémoires* 13 (2000), 3–200

Effenberger A., 'Überlegungen zur Aufstellung des Theodosius-Obelisken im Hippodrom von Konstantinopel' in B. Brenk (ed.), *Innovation in der Spätantike* (Wiesbaden: Reichert, 1996), 207–82

'Zu den beiden Reiterstandbildern auf dem Tauros von Konstantinopel', *Millennium* 5 (2008), 261–97

'Zur Wiederverwendung der venezianischen Tetrarchengruppen in Konstantinopel', *Millennium* 10 (2013), 215–74

Floren J., 'Zu Lysipps Statuen des sitzenden Herakles', *Boreas* 4 (1981), 47–60

Frickenhaus A., 'Der Eros von Myndos', *Jahrbuch des Deutschen Archäologischen Instituts* 30 (1915), 127–29

Gehn U. and B. Ward-Perkins, 'Constantinople', in R. R. R. Smith and B. Ward-Perkins (eds.), *The Last Statues of Antiquity* (Oxford: Oxford University Press 2016), 136–45

Griebeler A., 'The Serpent Column and the talismanic ecologies of Byzantine Constantinople', *Byzantine and Modern Greek Studies* 44 (2019), 86–105

Guberti Bassett S., 'Historiae custos: sculpture and tradition in the Baths of Zeuxippos', *American Journal of Archaeology* 100 (1996), 491–506

Gyllius P., *De topographia Constantinopoleos* (Lyon: Rovillius, 1561)

James L., 'Pray not to fall into temptation and be your own guard: pagan statues in Christian Constantinople', *Gesta* 35 (1996), 12–20

Jouette J.-C., 'Divination, magie et sorcellerie autour des statues antiques et des colonnes historiées de Constantinople (XIe–XIIe siècles)' in V. Dasen and J.-M. Spieser (eds.), *Les savoirs magiques et leur transmission de l'Antiquité à la Renaissance*. Micrologus' Library 60 (Florence: SISMEL, 2014), 461–75

Kaldellis A., 'Christodoros on the statues of the Zeuxippos baths: a new reading of the *Ekphrasis*', *Greek, Roman and Byzantine Studies* 47 (2007), 361–83

Keesling C. M., 'Greek statue terms revisited: what does ἀνδριάς mean?' *Greek, Roman and Byzantine Studies* 57 (2017), 836–61

Kiilerich B., 'The Barletta Colossus revisited', *Acta ad Archaeologiam et Artivm Historiam Pertinentia* 28 (2015), 55–72

Kirfel W., *Die dreiköpfige Gottheit* (Bonn: Dümmler, 1948)

Konrad C., 'Beobachtungen zur Architektur und Stellung des Säulenmonuments in Istanbul-Cerrahpasa "Arkadiussäule"', *Istanbuler Mitteilungen* 51 (2001), 319–401

Laubscher H. P., 'Beobachtungen zu tetrarchischen Kaiserbildnissen aus Porphyr', *Jahrbuch des Deutschen Archäologischen Instituts* 44 (1999), 207–52

Leeb R., *Konstantin und Christus*, Arbeiten zur Kirchengeschichte 58 (Berlin: De Gruyter, 1992)

Lehmann P. W., 'Theodosius or Justinian? A Renaissance drawing of a Byzantine rider?', *Art Bulletin* 41 (1959), 39–57

Loverance R., 'The bronze goose from the Hippodrome' in Shilling and Stephenson, *Fountains*, 87–102

Magdalino P., 'The End of Time in Byzantium' in Brandes and Schmieder, *Endzeiten*, 119–33

Majeska G. P., *Russian Travelers to Constantinople in the Fourteenth and Fifteenth Centuries*, Dumbarton Oaks Studies 19 (Washington: Dumbarton Oaks, 1984)

Mango C., 'Antique statuary and the Byzantine beholder', *Dumbarton Oaks Papers* 17 (1963), 53–75

'The columns of Justinian and his successors' in *Studies on Constantinople* (Aldershot: Ashgate, 1997), X 1–20

'Constantine's porphyry column and the Chapel of St Constantine', *Deltion tes Christianikes Archaiologikes Hetaireias* 4, 10 (1981), 103–10

'Epigrammes honorifiques, statues et portraits a Byzance' in *Studies on Constantinople* (Aldershot: Ashgate 1997), IX 22–35

'Septime Severe et Byzance', *Comptes rendus des séances de l'Académie de Inscriptions et Belles-Lettres* 147 (2003), 593–608

Mango C., M. Vickers, and E. D. Francis, 'The Palace of Lausus at Constantinople and its collection of ancient statues', *Journal of the History of Collections* 4 (1992), 89–98

Martins de Jesus C. A., 'The nude Constantinople: masterpieces of Greek sculpture at Byzantium according to the Greek Anthology' in R. Morais, D. Leão, D. Rodríguez Pérez and D. Ferreira (eds.), *Greek Art in Motion: Studies in Honour of Sir John Boardman on the Occasion of His 90th Birthday* (Oxford: Archaeopress Archaeology, 2019), 78–84

'The statuary collection held at the baths of Zeuxippus (Ap 2) and the search for Constantine's museological intentions', *Synthesis* 21 (2014), www.memoria.fahce.unlp.edu.ar/art_revistas/pr.6391/pr.6391.pdf

Mathiopulu E., 'Klassisches und Klassizistisches im Statuenfragment von Niketas Choniates', *Byzantinische Zeitschrift* 73 (1980), 25–40

Naumann R., 'Der antike Rundbau beim Myrelaion und der Palast Romanos I. Lekapenos', *Istanbuler Mitteilungen* 16 (1966), 199–216

'Neue Beobachtungen am Theodosiusbogen und Forum Tauri in Istanbul', *Istanbuler Mitteilungen* 26 (1976), 117–41

Newskaja W. P., *Byzanz in der klassischen und hellenistischen Epoche* (Leipzig: Koehler & Amelang, 1955)

Niewöhner P. and J. Abura, 'Der frühbyzantinische Rundbau beim Myrelaion in Konstantinopel. Kapitelle, Mosaiken und Ziegelstempel', *Istanbuler Mitteilungen* 60 (2010), 411–59

Niewöhner P. and U. Peschlow, 'Neues zu den Tetrarchenfiguren in Venedig und zu ihrer Aufstellung in Konstantinopel', *Istanbuler Mitteilungen* 62 (2012), 341–67

Odorico P., 'Du recueil à l'invention du texte: le cas des Parastaseis syntomoi chronikai', *Byzantinische Zeitschrift* 107 (2014), 755–84

Papamastorakis T., 'Interpreting the *de Signis* of Nicetas Choniates' in A. Simpson and S. Efthymiadis (eds.), *Nicetas Choniates: A Historian and a Writer* (Geneva: La pomme d'or, 2009), 209–22

Peschlow U., 'Eine wiedergewonnene byzantinische Ehrensäule in Istanbul', in O. Feld and U. Peschlow (eds.), *Studien zur spätantiken und byzantinischen Kunst. Festschrift für F. W. Deichmann*, Monographien des Römisch-germanisches Zentralmuseum 10.1 (Bonn: Habelt, 1986), 23–33

Pingitzer P., 'Nilpferd attackiert Krokodil. Zur Darstellung einer Tierkampfszene auf einer Gemme aus Carnuntum', *Forum Archaeologiae* 87/VI/2018, http://farch.net

Pont A.-V., 'Septime Sévère à Byzance: l'invention d'un fondateur', *Antiquité Tardive* 18 (2010), 191–198

Poulsen E., 'A bronze portrait statuette of the Sovereign-Sun of about 500 AD (Theoderic?)' in J. Arce and F. Burkhalter (eds.), *Bronce y religion romana. Actas del XI Congreso internacional de bronces antiguos* (Madrid: Consejo Superior de Investigaciones Científicas, 1993), 349–60

Puech V., 'Les statues des bains de Zeuxippe à Constantinople: collection et patrimoine dans l'Antiquité tardive', *Anabasis* 24 (2016), 145–81

Russell T., *Byzantium and the Bosporus* (Oxford: Oxford University Press, 2017)

Saradi H., 'Christodorus of Koptus, the statuary of the baths of Zeuxippus: Virgilian heroes in a Constantinopolitan context' in Ch. Chotzakoglu (ed.): *Ζείδωρος Ὑετός* (Levkosia: Hetaireia Kypriakon Spoudon, 2019), II 703–18

Schreiner P., 'Untersuchungen zu den Niederlassungen westlicher Kaufleute im Byzantinischen Reich des 11. und 12. Jahrhunderts', *Byzantinische Forschungen* 7 (1979), 175–91

Shilling B. and P. Stephenson, *Fountains and Water Culture in Byzantium* (Cambridge: Cambridge University Press, 2016)

Speck P., 'War Bronze ein knappes Metall? Die Legende von dem Stier auf dem Bus in den 'Parastaseis 42'', *Hellenika* 39 (1988), 3–17

Stephenson P., *The Serpent Column: A Cultural Biography* (New York: Oxford University Press, 2016)

'The Serpent Column fountain' in Shilling and Stephenson, *Fountains*, 103–29

Stichel R., 'Die Schlangensäule im Hippodrom von Istanbul', *Istanbuler Mitteilungen* 47 (1997), 315–48

Striker C. L., *The Myrelaion, Bodrum Camii, in Istanbul* (Princeton: Princeton University Press, 1981)

Stupperich R., 'Das Statuenprogramm in den Zeuxippos-Thermen. Überlegungen zur Beschreibung durch Christodoros von Koptos', *Istanbuler Mitteilungen* 32 (1982), 210–35

Thomov T., 'The last column in Constantinople', *Byzantinoslavica* 59 (1998), 80–91

Tissoni F., *Cristodoro. Un'introduzione e un commento* (Alessandria: Edizioni Dell'Orso, 2000)

Van der Vin J. P., *Travellers to Greece and Constantinople: Ancient Monuments and Old Traditions in Medieval Travellers' Tales*, Uitgaven van het Nederlands Historisch-Archeologisch Instituut te Istanbul 49 (Istanbul: Nederlands Historisch-Archaeologisch Instituut te Istanbul, 1980)

Von Mosch H.-C., 'Hadrians "Sandalenlöser". Der Hermes des Lysipp (?) auf den Münzen von Trapezous, Amastris und Markianopolis', *Jahrbuch für Numismatik und Geldgeschichte* 63 (2013), 93–149

'Aphrodite Selene. Von der Aenadon genetrix zum problematischen Bios der Helena Augusta', *Jahrbuch für Numismatik und Geldgeschichte* 67 (2017), 145–239

Von Schlosser J., 'Kleinasiatische und thrakische Münzbilder der Kaiserzeit', *Numismatische Zeitschrift* 23 (1891), 1–28

Whitby M., 'Christodorus of Coptus on the statues in the Baths of Zeuxippus at Constantinople: text and context' in *Nonnus of Panopolis in Context II: Poetry, Religion, and Society*, Mnemosyne, Supplement 408 (Leiden: Brill, 2017), 271–88

Williams R., *Arius: Heresy and Tradition* (Grand Rapids, Michigan: Eerdmans, 2001)

Cambridge Elements ≡

The History of Constantinople

Peter Frankopan
University of Oxford

Peter Frankopan is Professor of Global History at Oxford University, where he is also Director of the Centre for Byzantine Research and Senior Research Fellow at Worcester College. He specialises in the history of the Eastern Mediterranean from antiquity to the modern day, and is the author of the bestsellers *The Silk Roads: A New History of the World* (2015) and *The New Silk Roads: The Future and Present of the World* (2018).

About the Series
Telling the history of Constantinople through its monuments and people, leading scholars present a rich and unbiased account of this ever-evolving metropolis. From its foundation to the domination of the Ottoman Empire to contemporary Istanbul, numerous aspects of Constantinople's narrative are explored in this unrivalled series.

Cambridge Elements $\equiv$

The History of Constantinople

Elements in the Series

The Statues of Constantinople
Albrecht Berger

A full series listing is available at: www.cambridge.org/EHCO

Printed in the United States
by Baker & Taylor Publisher Services